Life-Writing

Biography Monographs
published for the Biographical Research Center
by the University of Hawai'i Press

Life-Writing: A Glossary of Terms in Biography, Autobiography, and Related Forms,
by Donald J. Winslow. 1980. 2nd ed. 1995.
*New Directions in Biography: Essays by Phyllis Auty, Leon Edel, Michael Holroyd,
Noel C. Manganyi, Gabriel Merle, Margot Peters, and Shoichi Saeki,* edited and
with a Foreword by Anthony M. Friedson. 1981.
Essaying Biography: A Celebration for Leon Edel, edited by Gloria G. Fromm.
1986.
The Autobiographical Writings of Lewis Mumford: A Study in Literary Audacity, by
Frank G. Novak, Jr. 1988.
Called from Within: Early Women Lawyers of Hawai'i, edited by Mari Matsuda.
1992.
A Man Must Stand Up: The Autobiography of a Gentle Activist, by John E.
Reinecke, edited by Alice M. Beechert and Edward D. Beechert. 1993.

The Center for Biographical Research (CBR) of the University of Hawai'i is
designed to facilitate and encourage the study of life-writing. Founded in
1976, CBR sponsors research, publication, teaching, and service for the
pan-cultural study of biography. In addition to the scholarly journal
Biography: An Interdisciplinary Quarterly, published continuously since 1978,
the Center produces a series of book-length monographs on topics in life-
writing. In conjunction with the University's Liberal Studies program, CBR
offers an undergraduate interdisciplinary major in biography, and in conjunction with the English Department, graduate programs leading to M.A.
and Ph.D. degrees with a specialization in biography. Since 1988 the Center
has hosted a weekly seminar, "Brown Bag Biography," featuring discussions
of biography for town and gown, and has sponsored international confer-
ences in biography in Kyoto and Chiangmai, as well as Honolulu. For further information about the programs or activities of the Center, please con-
tact the: Center for Biographical Research; University of Hawai'i at Mānoa;
1777 East-West Road, Cottage 96-36; Honolulu, Hawai'i 96822; telephone
and fax: (808) 956-3774; email:simson@uhunix.uhcc.hawaii.edu.

Life-Writing

A GLOSSARY OF TERMS IN BIOGRAPHY, AUTOBIOGRAPHY, AND RELATED FORMS
Second Edition

Donald J. Winslow

A Biography Monograph
*Published for the Biographical Research Center by
University of Hawai'i Press*

Library of Congress Cataloging-in-Publication Data
Winslow, Donald J., 1911–
Life-writing : a glossary of terms in biography, autobiography,
and related forms / Donald J. Winslow. — 2nd ed.
    p.   cm. — (A biography monograph)
Includes bibliographical references.
ISBN 0-8248-1713-3
1. Biography as a literary form—Dictionaries.
2. Autobiography—Dictionaries.
I. Title II. Series.
CT21.W56 1995
808'.06692—dc20   94–40735
CIP

University of Hawai'i Press books are printed on acid-free
paper and meet the guidelines for permanence and durability
of the Council on Library Resources

About the Author

DONALD J. WINSLOW is Professor Emeritus of English at Boston University, where he taught for forty-one years, ten of them as Chair of the English Department. In addition to many years of teaching courses on biography, he has specialized in eighteenth-century literature. His many articles in the *Thomas Hardy Journal* include a number on Hardy iconography, with special concern for Hardy's relationships to the artists who painted his portrait. He has also published *Lasell: A History of the First Junior College for Women* (1987), now a four-year college, an institution with which Professor Winslow has had a lifetime association.

Contents

Preface to the Second Edition

THE PRESENT REVISED edition of the Glossary alters or adds to a number of the earlier definitions while including more than one hundred new terms. In the fourteen years since publication of the first edition, the field of life-writing has expanded at a rapid rate. The multiplication of new books and articles on biography and autobiography has meant an expanded bibliography. Fortunately, the publication of the journal *Biography* has provided a major source for ever-new investigations into innumerable aspects of life-writing, including extensive bibliographical listings. New books on theory and criticism, especially in autobiography, have led to the introduction of new terms, some of which are of real value, while some add to the jargonizing of the language. I do not avoid neologisms, but here at least I do not encourage the use of jargon.

I have continued to resist the temptation to include terms relating to the professions of subjects of biographies. One could easily add scores of categories of this type, beginning with architects, book-sellers, and composers, but those subjects deserve much more than dictionary entries; they need articles, even books, dealing with the special problems and characteristics for each type. I try to confine myself to terms concerned with literary genres and with the general human condition.

I reiterate my gratitude to the University of Hawai'i Press and the University of Hawai'i Center for Biographical Research and its director, George Simson. I owe special thanks to Ira B. Nadel for his helpful suggestions and close reading of the entire text.

Auburndale, Massachusetts, 1994

Preface

THERE HAS LONG been need for a reference list of terms that are used in connection with biography, autobiography, and other branches of life-writing. Since this glossary was gathered over a period of many years during which I was teaching courses in biography at Boston University, the bias of the collection is British and American. Other languages and cultures await other collectors of lists of terms and definitions.

Any glossary such as this is easily extendable, and one has to make certain limitations within reason. It would be pleasant to include, for example, all the various double terms for the many different professions as subjects of biography, like "merchant lives" or "artists' lives," but such terms are clearly evident in meaning. One could write an essay on such topics as "ecclesiastical lives" (of which there are probably more than of any other profession) or "medical lives" (an especially interesting group since the seventeenth century), but these subjects need considerably more than definition. Some large terms are included here, such as "history" or "narrative," but they are defined or discussed only in relation to the basic subject of the collection: life-writing.

Many different sources have been used, but the main definitions are from the *Oxford English Dictionary* (OED). I have used other dictionaries and also books and articles from recent times that define and discuss many of these terms. At the end of the book is a selected bibliography of books on life-writing, mainly general studies, although some concentrate on specific writers who are representative. Although most of the books listed are from the contemporary period, some of the very earliest studies in biography are included, partly to indicate something of the progress that has been made over the last century in dealing with theories and practices of biography and autobiography. The bibliography might have been greatly extended by including such works as dictionaries of lives or anthologies of passages from lives, but one must draw lines of limitation somewhere. The journal *Biography,* in which this glossary was originally published, has in its last number each year a bibliography of current books and articles on life-writing.

In selecting terms for a list such as this, one is sometimes faced with the problem of deciding whether or not to include a term that is highly idiosyncratic. Daily journalism often provides new words or phrases in order to vivify an account of some biographer or his work. Book reviewers attempt originality in their metaphors, sometimes hitting—often missing—the mark. Many terms have been used so widely and for so long that they are no longer really metaphorical (they are "faded metaphors" at best), like "profile" or "sketch," but still they are effective designations of literary types. These and other metaphors for life-writing understandably come from the field of painting portraits ("silhouette," "vignette"), yet there is one apt metaphorical analogy that has only occasionally been used: mosaic. One can see how the little hard pieces of fact (the tesserae) have to be fitted together to make a complete picture of the person. Selection is such an inevitable part of all biography and autobiography that the parallel of the life-writer to the artist in mosaic stresses the importance of choice and arrangement, of pattern and design.

Some concepts associated with life-writing, though influential and popular at one historical period or another (astrology, humors, phrenology, biorhythm), go in or out of fashion or pass away, having been attempts to understand basic human nature and to apply theoretical principles to specific individuals. Obviously in the twentieth century the field of psychology (Freudian, Jungian, Adlerian, Eriksonian, or whatever) has brought in many terms—some now entirely familiar, others still coming in. Not unexpectedly, there are controversies not only on the specific meanings of these new terms but also on the very basic concepts out of which they continue to grow.

If autobiography is the major subject of discussion in books and articles in the last generation, perhaps the next most frequent topic is the fact-fiction interfusion. Ever since the eighteenth century the relationship between the novel and biography has been intimate and complex; many recent scholarly studies have dealt with these interrelationships, often when the subject is a specific author. Obviously, then, many of the terms here included are applicable to the literature of fiction as well as to that of fact, and some modern terms are created in order to distinguish between fiction and fact.

Creative artists invent new forms, sometimes unconsciously, and these in turn bring in a new vocabulary that is often, especially at first, ambiguous or unclear. Use makes for clarity—at least one hopes so. But even the basic terms, like "history" or "fiction," may come under close examination by critical minds, and over and over again scholars argue over definition or classification. A compiler of glossaries has to be aware of the ambiguities and the critical controversies, but ultimately he must make his own decision on definition and illustration, for it is by example that the definer can perhaps best clarify meaning.

Life-writing has its own particular history in the development of a critical vocabulary. The words "biography" and "autobiography" came into the English language very late, and it is largely in the eighteenth and in the twentieth centuries that new words and terms have accumulated in relation to life-writing. There are those who, to this day, find the term "life-writing" unfamiliar. It is of Anglo-Saxon origin, as opposed to the Greek-Latin origin of the more familiar terms, but "life-writing" was used as early as the eighteenth century, and it does seem to be a more inclusive term than "biography." At least that is the way in which I use it here. One word has yet to be discovered or invented: a term, comparable to "historiography" or "poetics," for the study of biography.

I acknowledge the aid of the University of Hawai'i and the Biographical Research Center in publishing this glossary. George Simson, editor of *Biography*, has been of great assistance to me throughout. In particular I thank my wife, Charlotte, for her advice and aid and I dedicate this and all my work to her.

Boston, 1980

Glossary

A

account. A narrative relation of events in a life, or lives; frequently used in titles before the word **biography** was in general use; *account* implies a methodical treatment of a life (e.g., Gerard Langbaine, *An Account of the English Dramatick Poets*, 1691; Nicholas Rowe, *Account of the Life of Shakespeare*, 1709).

acta sanctorum. Acts of the saints. See **hagiography.**

adventures. A sequence of exciting, remarkable incidents or events; a term often used in titles of biographies or autobiographies of a sensational or romantic sort (e.g., *The Life and Adventures of Matthew Bishop*, 1744; Edward Trelawny, *Adventures of a Younger Son*, 1831).

adversary portrait. In the general class of negative biographies, but suggesting a specific personal attack on an already published biography of the eulogistic type. See **vituperative biography.**

aet. or **aetatis.** (L. *aetatis suae*, in a certain year of one's age.) At the age of; often placed in the corner of a portrait indicating the age of the subject at the time the portrait was painted.

African American life-writing. Lives of blacks written by blacks, in America; also includes some lives of blacks written by whites. Beginning with slave narratives, before the Civil War and later, the development of African American life-writing was mainly in autobiography, from the pattern of rise in white society (Frederick Douglass, Booker T. Washington), to more penetrating analysis of black alienation in a hostile environment (Richard Wright, Angelo Herndon), and major late twentieth-century lives, some in series of autobiographies (Maya Angelou), some strongly political (Malcolm X), and with outstanding literary quality (James Baldwin). Popular figures have written personal accounts (Ethel Waters, Lena Horn), often with assistance from professional journalists. Probably the most influential African American life in the late twentieth century is Alex Haley's *Roots*, partly because of its successful TV series, a work which not only influenced black life-writing but all lives involved in searching for ancestry. The progress from protest literature to more sophisticated cultural studies, revealing psychological and philosophical

1

knowledge, has made African American life-writing a major phase of contemporary literature. See **black life-writing, slave narrative.**

-ana. A termination, or word, indicating a miscellaneous collection of anecdotes, incidents, writings, reflections, table talk, etc., of an eminent or interesting individual. Used in French in the sixteenth and seventeenth centuries and in English by the late seventeenth and early eighteenth centuries for scraps of information, or gossip, about persons or places of note. A favorite form in eighteenth century England, showing the rise of interest in the anecdote, with innumerable collections of sayings, literary trifles, society verses, clever sayings, etc. (e.g., *Walpoliana, Boswelliana, Thraliana*). Robert Southey called Boswell's *Life of Johnson* the *Ana* of all *Anas*. See **anecdote, dicta, opinions, scrappiana, table talk.**

anecdote. The narrative of a detached incident, or of a single event, told as being in itself interesting, striking, revealing; secret, private, or hitherto unpublished brief narratives of details in the history of a life, illustrative of one or more aspects of an individual character or personality. The anecdote came into prominence in the eighteenth century, reaching a peak of popularity at the end of the century, partly as a result of the influence of Samuel Johnson as a subject of anecdotes and of Boswell as a retailer of anecdotes. The popularity of the form has continued through the nineteenth century to the present day, often associated with certain major personalities (Lincoln, Churchill) and with those professions that seem to encourage the anecdote (theatre, cinema, politics, public performers of all kinds). Certain personalities seem to have encouraged the spreading of anecdotes about themselves, as for example George Bernard Shaw, and perhaps even Samuel Johnson himself. (Joseph Spence, *Anecdotes*, 1820; Hester Thrale Piozzi, *Anecdotes of the Late Samuel Johnson*, 1786; Horace Walpole, *Anecdotes of Painting*, 1762.)

annals. Records of events year by year, of historical events generally; formal reports of learned societies presented as yearly records. The Annales school of historians, originated in France in 1929 by Lucien Febre and Marc Bloch, were opposed to political narrative and instead stressed themes or trends, especially economic and social ones. Such serial history was often involved in statistical studies, another aspect of quantitative history. Economic historians, as well as other social scientists, were concerned with serial and quantitative history, and have been greatly assisted by the development of the computer. Parallel concerns in biography become evident in the same mid-twentieth century period. See **chronicle, prosopography.**

antiquarian. See **biographical dictionary.**

apology. See **autobiography.**

archives. A place where public records or other historic documents are kept; records so preserved. Collections of family papers, genealogical records, etc. James Boswell used to refer to his private papers at his home in Auchinleck as his archives.

authenticity. See **documentation.**

authorized biography. A life written by a biographer who has been chosen or approved by the person or persons who have authority over the subject's estate or literary remains, possibly a surviving family member or executor. Occasionally a living subject authorizes a biographer. The term is often used as a means of giving the reader the sense that this particular life is more authentic than any other. Authorization can become a highly complex affair: see Janet Malcolm's "The Silent Woman" (*New Yorker,* August 23 and 30, 1993), a three-part account of the turmoils of five or more biographers of Sylvia Plath and their difficulties with authorization. See **life** *(official, standard),* **unauthorized biography.**

autobibliographer. A term coined by Theodore Besterman to describe a person who has compiled a bibliography of his own works.

autobiographical collage. Another original term related to the art of painting that suggests fragments placed together to present a unified whole; autobiographers often include only bits and pieces of their lives put together as one might do a collage; the term has been used by Kurt Vonnegut.

autobiography. The writing of one's own history; the story of one's life written by oneself. Although the term was first used by a reviewer (possibly William Taylor) in the British *Monthly Review* (1797) and in 1809 by Robert Southey, there have been true autobiographies from ancient times onward (see Georg Misch, *A History of Autobiography in Antiquity,* 2 vols., 1907, revised 1931, translated from the German, 1949, 1959). Before the term was introduced such words as *apologia,* **apology, confessions,** and **memoirs** were used. The term **apology** suggests a defense, or vindication, although there is also a disarming tone of humility and an implication of frankness and honesty. It was popular in titles of eighteenth century autobiographies (e.g., Colley Cibber, *Apology for his Life,* 1740; *Apology for the Life of George Anne Bellamy,* 1785). Cardinal Newman's *Apologia pro Vita sua* (1864) is principally concerned with his spiritual life. The term **confessions,** as in the *Confessions of St. Augustine,* implies an acknowledgment of one's sins, faults, wrongdoings, or weaknesses. It is, of course, derived from the religious act of confession to a priest as a religious duty, yet it also derives from the idea of confession of faith, or conversion (as in St. Augustine). In more modern times, especially after Rousseau's *Confessions* (1781), the term takes on a more worldly, less spiritual, meaning, often with the implication of shocking or scandalous revelations (e.g., Thomas De Quincey, *Confessions of an English Opium Eater,*

1822). It may even be used with humorous overtones. Since Freud the term has taken on the atmosphere of the psychiatrist's couch rather than of the confessional stall. The idea of repentance is lost in sensational exhibitionism and boasting. In *British Autobiography in the Seventeenth Century* Paul Delany uses the term "ad hoc autobiography" to describe an autobiography "motivated by its author's involvement in a major political issue, or by his desire to exploit some temporary notoriety," a kind of testimony relating to a specific political event. Autobiography in the nineteenth century is marked by major individual works (John Stuart Mill, Cardinal Newman, Anthony Trollope, Henry Adams), and in the twentieth century it has become a pervasive aspect of all literature, partly as a result of psychological advances and partly as a reflection of the desire of the individual to fight against being submerged by impersonal bureaucracy and mass guidance; the name fights for recognition over the computerized number. Not only are autobiographers more active than ever, but the major literary forms of poetry, novel, and drama are heavy with confessional and autobiographical materials and methods, from Proust, Joyce, D. H. Lawrence, and Philip Roth to Arthur Miller, Robert Lowell, Sylvia Plath, and John Updike, to name only a few. Books and articles presenting various theories on autobiography have proliferated beyond what anyone would have expected when in 1909 Anna Robeson Burr published *The Autobiography: A Critical and Comparative Study,* then a remarkably new subject for special study. In the last years of the twentieth century scholarly research on autobiography has outrun that on biography; the work of James Olney and many others has made advances far beyond what might have been anticipated a few decades ago. See **book of, diary, journal, memoirs, memorials, recollections, reminiscences, spiritual autobiography.**

autogynography. Writing by women about themselves; a term used by Germaine Bree and by Donna C. Stanton in her essay so titled in *The Female Autograph* (1984). See **feminist life-writing.**

autohagiography. A self-explanatory word, probably most useful in a humorous vein for the autobiographer who portrays himself as a saint; e.g., the *Times Literary Supplement* review (June 26, 1992) of Derek Jarman, *At Your Own Risk: A Saint's Testament.* See **hagiography.**

automythology. A myth or pattern of myths used by an autobiographer to give form to his life story. An interesting example is Edwin Muir's autobiography. See **myth.**

autonovel. A term used by David Leitch for his own account of himself in *God Stand Up For Bastards* (1973). It seems to suggest a reflection of one's self through other persons, as in Harold Nicolson's *Some*

People (1927), Max Beerbohm's *Seven Men* (1919), or Julian Symons's *Notes From Another Country* (1972). This term might, however, be applied to any strongly autobiographical novel.

autoportrait. An unusual term for autobiographical writing, suggesting a self-image comparable to that of an artist's self-portrait. Used by Michel Beaujour in his *Miroirs d'encre: Rhétorique de l'auto-portrait* (1980).

B

bibliography of biography. Lists of biographies have been made from early times, but more recently scholarly indexes, serial publications (some intermittently published), and professional or occupational lists of lives and dictionaries of biography have been issued. As early as 1934 Phyllis Riches published *An Analytic Bibliography of Universal Collected Biography*, and more recent bibliographies have appeared in foreign languages as well as in English. In 1986 the second edition of *Biographical Dictionaries and Related Works*, edited by Robert B. Slocum, was published. Current listings are to be found in the cumulative indexes of the journal *Biography*, published in the fourth number (Fall) of each volume. The most massive biographical bibliography is that published by Gale Research, *Biography and Genealogy Master Index*, a multivolume edition of biographical dictionaries continually being published from the mid-1980s on, and currently available in a variety of electronic and "hard copy" formats. See **biographical dictionary.**

bio-bibliography. As originally used by Southey in 1809, dealing with the life and writings of an author; as used by Frederick A. Pottle in 1965 (Note to 2nd Impression, *The Literary Career of James Boswell*, xxvi), the chronological, detailed bibliography of an author as preparatory to the biography. As Pottle says, "the biography of an author is best approached through bio-bibliography." Also a combination of biography and bibliography (e.g., D. C. Dickinson, *A Bio-Bibliography of Langston Hughes*, 1972). One of the most extensive examples of the chronological examination of an author's life through his publications is Gillian Fenwick's *Leslie Stephen's Life in Letters: A Bibliographical Study* (1993), a work which creates what may well be called a new form of biography. See **chronology.**

biodigm. A term created by George Simson in 1982 to describe biographical paradigms—"declensions of judgment about biography.

Each biodigm is a complex factor in a mimetic equation comprising those connections between a life led and the writing constructed to represent that life. The most important biodigms are that biography is a record of mortality, that it is a fact-conditioned art, and that the judgment of biography is governed by multiple, compatible criteria."

biografiction. A pejorative term used by Durling and Watt (*Biography: Varieties and Parallels*, 1941) to describe fictionalized biography in the 1920s. See **biographical novel.**

biographee. One who is the subject of a biography; probably first used in the early nineteenth century, now much more frequently used, especially in relation to the subjects in *Who's Who* and similar publications.

biographia. Before the word **biography** came into the language in the late seventeenth century, the word *biographia*, for the writing of lives, was fairly common. The word was retained in the eighteenth century as a title for collections of lives *(Biographia Classica, Biographia Dramatica)*, when latinate titles were still popular; the most important of these was the *Biographia Britannica*, covering the lives of all eminent Englishmen, published from 1747 to 1795; this work was the forerunner of the *Dictionary of National Biography*. The words *biographus* and *biograph* were rare, though they meant biographical sketch or notice; they are now obsolete terms. The word *biographer*, the writer of lives, was used as early as 1715 in Addison's *Freeholder*. The word *biographiable*, though used at least once in a letter by Rupert Brooke, is an unusual construction.

biographical anthology. This term may simply describe a volume of short biographies (e.g., Marston Balch, ed., *Modern Short Biographies and Autobiographies*, 1935), or selections from major biographies (e.g., Edgar Johnson, ed., *A Treasury of Biography*, 1941); both of these books were widely used as texts in biography courses in American colleges. More recently it has been used and defined in a narrower sense (*Times Literary Supplement*, December 21, 1973) in a review of *Landor: A Biographical Anthology* as "that new literary hybrid . . . a species of book in which are alternated slices of biography with excerpts from the writings that were done during the period of the biographical slice that precedes them."

biographical dictionary. A book of information or reference, in alphabetical order, on individual lives. Biographical dictionaries really began with the lists of antiquarians in the sixteenth century. John Leyland, King's Antiquary, 1533, under Henry VIII saved much material from the despoiled monasteries, and John Bale, Leyland's contemporary, made lists of English writers and helped to preserve factual material used by later historians. In the seventeenth century John Aubrey's *Brief Lives* was more a disorganized collection of facts and anecdotes than a dictionary. The founding of the Society of Antiquarians in 1717 helped further this work and in the eighteenth century biographical dictionaries came into their own (*Biographia Britannica*, 1747–1795). The major biographical dictionary in England is the *Dictionary of National Biography* (DNB), begun in 1882, edited by Leslie Stephen till 1889, then by Sir Sidney Lee (1889–1901). In his *Studies of a Biographer*, Stephen discusses his purpose and methods in a series of essays. The DNB includes biographies from the beginning to 1900 of all national notabilities who are no longer living. Supplements to the DNB were issued and a concise DNB was published. The work continues to be added to; it is an indispensable source book containing in its original twenty-seven volumes over thirty thousand names. The American equivalent is the *Dictionary of American Biography* (DAB), originally published in twenty volumes (1928–1936), whose best known editor was Dumas Malone. Neither the DNB nor the DAB includes living persons. The DAB contains fourteen thousand lives by over two thousand contributors; supplements are published. In the twentieth century scores of biographical dictionaries have been published, alphabetical listings of names and factual information for various professions, social classes, and periods of time, including the living in *Who's Who* (British) and *Who's Who in America*, published annually. Probably the most widely used biographical dictionary is *Webster's New Biographical Dictionary*. Reprinted and revised over twenty times since first publication in the 1940s, the work now contains over thirty thousand brief entries, including "lives of celebrated, important or notorious men and women ... from all parts of the world, all eras, and all fields of endeavor." The multiplication of biographical dictionaries has brought forth many weak and inadequate collections as well as the authoritative, useful works. See **Who's Who.**

biographical fallacy. Analogous to the "pathetic fallacy," a reading into a life one's own life, or misreading a literary subject's works as though they were straight autobiography; using the subject of a biography as a means of autobiography. These two rather different interpretations of the phrase indicate the varying ways in which the term has been, though infrequently, used.

biographical industry. So many lives of the same subject have multiplied over recent years that the term "industry" has frequently been applied to favorite literary subjects, from the Great Romantics (e.g., Wordsworth, Byron, Shelley, Keats) to major moderns (e.g., Hemingway, Joyce, Faulkner). The term also applies to work that is other than biographical or includes biography, such as the long-standing recognition of the "Boswell industry" at Yale University. The publishing of biographies and autobiographies has increased constantly in the latter decades of the twentieth century, as any glance at the R. R. Bowker *Publishers Weekly* reports indicates: August 9, 1993, for example, lists 131 lives, published by 81 presses. Books and articles on life-writing have multiplied, too, as the quarterly bibliographies in the journal *Biography* reveal.

biographical novel. The mixture of fact and fiction is as old in life-writing as it is in history. Since the novel and biography, as independent genres, developed together in the eighteenth century, it is not surprising that they influenced each other. Most early novels were written as though they were biographies or autobiographies (e.g., *The History of Tom Jones, A Foundling; The Adventures of Caleb Williams or Things as They Are*); the novelist in his desire to simulate the truth "deceived" the reader, and the reader "willingly suspended his disbelief." The realistic novel, from *Robinson Crusoe* to *Emma*, is obviously based on the biographical method. The historical novel is a genre of its own, especially popular in the nineteenth and early twentieth centuries. In the twentieth century it is sometimes difficult to distinguish the biographical novel from the novelized biography. Since Andrè Maurois's *Ariel: A Shelley Romance* (1923), a work Maurois himself later wished he had not published, the fictionalizing of biography has become almost a major industry, reaching a climax in the indefatigable work of Irving Stone *(Lust for Life; The Agony and the Ecstasy)*. Works such as those by Howard Fast, Catherine Drinker Bowen, Marchette Chute, Mary Renault, and others are often closer to the novel than to biography. In recent years some serious attempts in this genre have been made (e.g., Bruce Duffy's *The World As I Found It,* 1987, on Wittgenstein, and Susan Sontag's *Volcano Lover,* 1992, on Sir William Hamilton, Lady Hamilton, and Lord Nelson). A number of novelists are using biography and autobiography in ever increasing amounts (e.g,. Peter Ackroyd), or are portraying fictional characters involved in the problems of writing biography (e.g., Alison Lurie, Bernard Malamud). The Japanese admire a form called the I-Novel *(shishosetsu)*, a strongly autobiographical first person narrative (see John Lewell, *Modern Japanese Novelists: A Biographical Dictionary,* 1993).

biographobia. A relatively new term used to describe the fear, perhaps most obvious among writers, which many famous people have concerning their future biographers. Michael Millgate deals with this subject in his *Testamentary Acts* (1992).

biography. (*bios:* life, *graphein:* to write, from the Greek; *biographia,* from the Latin). Although the Latin and Greek forms of this word were used in antiquity, as an English word it is quite modern. The word *biographist* was used by Thomas Fuller in 1662, *biography* by Dryden in 1683, *biographer* by Addison in 1715, and *biographical* by

William Oldys in 1738. Samuel Johnson in his *Dictionary* defines *biographer* as "a writer of lives; a relater not of the history of nations, but of the actions of particular persons," and he quotes Addison: "Our Grubstreet biographers watch for the death of a great man, like so many undertakers, on purpose to make a penny of him." Johnson then defines biography only by quoting from Isaac Watts: "In writing the lives of men, which is called biography, some authors place every thing in precise order of time when it occurred." Johnson's most pertinent comments on life-writing are to be found in his *Rambler* No. 60 and in *Idler* No. 84. The usual definition is that biography is the history of the lives of individual people, as a branch of literature. Frequently quoted is Edmund Gosse's definition, "a faithful portrait of the soul in its adventures through life." It is the written record of the life of an individual; sometimes it is used to refer to the life course of other living creatures besides people—animals, or even plants— and even to inanimate phenomena, such as rivers. Some definitions are quite general: "the more or less formal and conscious recording of the life, or of a respectable fragment of the life, of an actual individual human being" (D. A. Stauffer). Some definers, in stressing the imaginative recreation, as well as the historical facts, stress the completeness of the life: "the simulation, in words, of a man's life, from all that is known about that man" (P. M. Kendall). Frank Brady (*Yale Review* 69, no. 1, 1979) divides biography into "two overlapping categories: ethical and mimetic;" the former "moves deductively" and the latter "moves inductively." He compares this distinction to Northrup Frye's between thematic and fictional literature. Ethical biography is sometimes called didactic. "Almost all biography up to the end of the eighteenth century is ethical...twentieth century biography tends to be highly mimetic." Until the word **autobiography** came into the language (1797), the word *biography* included the self-written life. Before the word *biography* came into the language the most frequent terms were **history,** or *history of the life of,* or **life.** See **autobiography, biographia, life, life-writing.**

biohistory. Historical writing from a biographical point of view; too general a term to mean only lives of "historical" figures; Thomas Carlyle's view of history as made up of the lives of great men, as in his *Heroes and Hero-Worship, and the Heroic in History* (1841). This concept of biography as essentially a branch of history was popular in the nineteenth century.

biometry. The calculation of the average duration and expectation of life; the measurement of life; biometer, a measurer of life.

bio-pic. A TIME-word meaning filmed biography, as in "Don Ameche's bio-pic of Alexander Graham Bell." Many late twentieth century films are biographical, with greatly varying success, from George C. Scott's performance as Patton to Ben Kingsley's portrayal of Gandhi. The word is sometimes spelled without the hyphen, as one word, a confusing practice because it misleads the pronunciation and the interpretation by making it seem like an optical term.

bios. A journalistic abbreviation for biographies, used especially by film and television personnel, particularly in relation to prepared material for an interviewer. The original Greek word *bios* means life.

bioscope. A view of life; that which affords such a view (e.g., W. Bayley, *Bagman's Bioscope:Various Views of Men and Manners,* 1824). Edmund Blunden (*Thomas Hardy,* 1992) coined the word *bioscopic,* meaning panoramic. See **cinematic.**

black life-writing. With the rise of black nationalism in Africa, both autobiographies and biographies are increasing in number. Before the twentieth century little but oral tradition of a heroic and poetic kind was evident on black lives. By the end of the 1950s a few autobiographies by black writers appeared, usually written in exile from South Africa and with their books banned there. Third World lives in general are likely to reflect race conflict and rising nationalism. Euro-African lives sometimes suggest a double life, and the black consciousness movement reveals both masking and protest. N. C. Manganyi, writing on black biography in South Africa (in Anthony Friedson, *New Directions in Biography,* 1981) speaks of "an undeclared moratorium on biography until such time as the South African political situation provides a greater climate of freedom and the dignity of individuals." He cites as examples of black autobiographers in the fifties and sixties Ezekiel Mphahlele, Peter Abrahams, Alfred Hutchinson, Ted Matshikiza, and Bloke Modisane. A remarkable black autobiography, Tepilit Ole Saitoti's *The Worlds of a Maasai Warrior* (1986), includes his years of education in America, where he earned both a bachelor's and a master's degree. He was unable to feel any closer to black Americans than he was to white, and when he returned to his tribe on the plains of the Serengeti, he was unable to explain Western culture to his family. American blacks have contributed widely to modern biographies and autobiographies, from Frederick Douglass and Booker T. Washington to Richard Wright and James Baldwin; see **African American life-writing.**

bon mot or **bons mots** (pl.). (Fr., literally "good word or words"). An especially apt or fitting word or phrase, a clever remark or witticism, repartee. For certain figures these are likely to be collected as representative, say, of wit or quick intelligence; often these are reported as having been heard in some social context, as with personalities like Oscar Wilde, George Bernard Shaw, Abraham Lincoln, or Winston Churchill. Frequently incorporated in anecdotes or serving as the climax to an anecdote. See **anecdote, table talk.**

book of. This phrase in the title of a biographical work generally indicates an early date of composition and may indicate religious material (*The Book of Margery Kempe,* 1436, pub. 1936; *The Book of Illustrious Henries,* 1446). If the work is modern, the title is probably a conscious attempt to give a flavor of antiquity.

brief lives. Though simply a descriptive term for short biographies, it has been identified with John Aubrey, whose *Brief Lives* were collected between 1669 and 1696, in part to supply material for Anthony Wood's *Athenae Oxoniensis,* a collection of lives of Oxford graduates. The factual accumulations and narrative interpretations of Aubrey's lives have made his work more memorable than Wood's dictionary. (See Oliver L. Dick, *Aubrey's Brief Lives,* 1949.) Aubrey's work contains about 130 lives, from the briefest few lines to several pages. His own life has been the subject of a popular play, *Brief Lives,* a one-person drama written and acted by Roy Dotrice.

C

calendar. See **hagiography.**

cameo. A metaphorical term used by Lytton Strachey, derived from the small jewel in which a face or figure is carved in relief on a different hued background, similar to miniature. Cameo portraits may be used in any life-writing, perhaps more especially in memoirs (political, social, or entertainment). Lillian Hellman's later autobiographical work (e.g., *Pentimento*) is noted for its cameo portraits. In biographical films brief appearances by historical personages are called "cameos." Strachey's *Portraits in Miniature* is made up of cameos.

campaign lives. A figurative expression for biographies that suggest any course of action analogous to a military campaign, especially political lives aimed at assisting a political candidate to win an election, to gain office (e.g., Hawthorne's *Life of Franklin Pierce,* 1852). The reverse of a campaign life is one written to denigrate a candidate. See **vituperative biography.**

canonicity. Originally a term related to biblical scholarship; used in relation to biographical material, authoritative or part of the genuine factual material of a person's life. Although it would be difficult to prove that there is a canon for works on biographical history and theory, such books as those by Richard Altick, Leon Edel, and David Novarr might be so classed in relation to British and American biography. Standards, rules, principles, and criteria for life-writing are still in the process of being established, if ever such canonization is possible. See **documentation, testamentary acts.**

caricature. A portrait or other artistic representation in which the characteristic features of the original are exaggerated with ludicrous effect; applied, by analogy, to life-writing of a distorted kind, deriving in part from the seventeenth century "character" and from satirical character sketches in eighteenth century poetry and prose (e.g., characters in the *Spectator,* in Pope's satiric poems, as "Atticus," "Sporus," etc.). In modern times the word is more frequently applied to pictorial art, cartoons, and the like, as in the work of Max Beerbohm; it has also been used in a condemnatory sense for certain biographies (e.g., Lytton Strachey's "Dr. Arnold" in *Eminent Victorians*).

case studies *(case histories).* Derived from the methodology of the Harvard Business School, and also from the development of Freudian and other schools of psychiatry; in life-writing "cases" may well have the intent of illustrating a particular type of character. Psychological case studies may provide the biographer in general with significant material for more "literary" art. See **psychoanalysis.**

celebiography. Another elision word for the life of a famous person, a celebrity ("lives of the rich and famous"); a term infrequently used, but a well-developed genre.

character. A genre derived from Theophrastus (d. 278 B.C.), the ancient Greek writer of generalized portraits of character types; only occasionally based on actual lives, the person is not described as an individual, but as a quality of virtue or vice, as "the good man," "the bad man," etc. Humors characters became popular in England after Joseph Hall's *Characters of Virtues and Vices* (1608); popular in the seventeenth century the form tended to disappear in the eighteenth, when the essay (e.g., Sir Roger de Coverley in the *Spectator*) and the novel absorbed the form. See **humors.**

character sketch. A description, or detailed report of a person's qualities; the estimate of a person's distinguishing features. The seventeenth century "character," strongly influenced by the popular concept of the four humors, exaggerated dominant characteristics. In the eighteenth century this form developed into the *character sketch,* as seen in the works of essayists like Steele and Addison. In life-writing the summarizing character sketch at the end of a biography is traditional in the eighteenth century, as in Boswell's *Life of Johnson,* and the custom continues into the nineteenth century. In modern times the character sketch is found occasionally in isolated form in magazines and newspapers, but it may also be found as an element within a larger work of biography or history. See **caricature, character, profile, silhouette, vignette.**

chirology. The science or art of determining personality from the characteristics of the hand, its shape and crease lines; distinguished from palmistry; part of the medical discipline of dermatoglyphics, which is concerned with the fine skin patterns (e.g., fingerprints) found on the hands and feet. See **hands.**

chronicle. A detailed and continuous register of events in order of time; a historical record, especially one in which the facts are narrated without philosophic treatment; a record, register, account. The chronicle was a characteristic form in medieval history and biography *(The Anglo-Saxon Chronicle).* Early royal lives written in England are mainly such chronicles of facts or events during the reign of the monarch (e.g., Bishop Asser's *Life of Alfred the Great,* 974). See **account, annals, chronology.**

chronique scandaleuse. (Fr. "scandalous chronicle"). A sensational story, often suggesting exaggeration or untruth. Popularly associated with court memoirs in France in the pre-Revolutionary period.

chronology. The arrangement of events in order of occurrence. The debate over the use of time sequence in life-writing recurs regularly, with the opposition reflected especially in the psychograph "invented" by Gamaliel Bradford, who used a topical approach. Perhaps the best defense of what is, in any case, the usual pattern of organization in life-writing is by Frederick A. Pottle in *The Literary Career of James Boswell* (1929), where by example he shows how a thorough chronology of a writer's works is indispensable before beginning a biography. The Macmillan Chronology Series, published until recently, assists biographers with this task. Examples of author chronologies are Norman Page, *A Dickens Chronology* (1984), Reginald Berry, *A Pope Chronology* (1988), and Jay Leyda, *The Melville Log,* 2 volumes (1951). See **bio-bibliography, log.**

cinematic. A technique or method in life-writing that involves an overall view of the background of a life; panoramic. A *cinematic biography* means a filmed life, or biographical cinema. In the 1930s and 1940s such films were especially popular (as in the portrayals of Disraeli by George Arliss and of Pasteur by Paul Muni) and usually undependable as to historical accuracy. The word *bioscopic,* meaning panoramic, was coined by Edmund Blunden (*Thomas Hardy,* 1942, 1951, p. 6): "According to current method, here should appear some bioscopic impression of the world in 1840 into which the subject of this volume arrived." Cinematic techniques are used in TV biographies, which have become more numerous and of better quality in the 1970s. Methods such as montage, rapid-fire sequences of pictures, often fading into one another, documentary background material, with brief interviews interspersed, and other devices have been used. The greatest advances and improvements appear to be in television. Some subjects are overdone because of their sensational appeal; witness the various JFK fantasies or *Malcolm X* by Spike Lee. Some notably successful cinematic lives, however, have been made (e.g., Richard Attenborough's *Gandhi* and Bernardo Bertolucci's *The Last Emperor*). See **docudrama.**

circumstantial biography. Lives written and published for special occasions, such as anniversaries, deaths, retirement, awards, and prizes, inspired by family desires for commemoration, publishers' wishes to capitalize on publicity, or professional biographers' concerns for success. Whether ceremony or scandal is the motive, such lives are produced by the circumstances of the time. Daniel Defoe in the early eighteenth century wrote pamphlet lives of criminals for sale to the crowds at Tyburn executions.

clerihew. Light verse dealing with a person; metrically uneven quatrains rhyming *aabb;* named for the British writer Edmund Clerihew Bentley (1875–1956), originator of this humorous, pseudobiographical verse; the name is always one of the rhymes (e.g., Sir Humphrey Davy / Abominated gravy / He lived in the odium / Of having discovered sodium). Bentley's nonsense verse appeared in *Biography for Beginners* (1905), *More Biography* (1929) and *Baseless Biography* (1939).

cliographer. Term invented by John Clive meaning the biographer of a historian.

cliometrics. The use of statistical methods in history; scientific techniques used in historical scholarship; quantitative studies; cf. econometrics.

collaboration. Working on a biography together; unusual in life-writing, but not unknown; for example, *Journey to the Frontier: Julian Bell and John Cornford: Their Lives and the 1930s,* by Peter Stansky and William Abrahams, although this extensive book could also be classed as **parallel lives.** In another sense the collaboration is that between the biographer and subject, especially in cases where the subject is still living. The relationship between biographer and subject can be anything from close collaboration to extreme antipathy. See **transference.**

collective lives. Works in which the lives of several, or many, persons are written for publication together, a method used in all times from antiquity to the present (Plutarch's *Lives,* Izaak Walton's *Lives,* Samuel Johnson's *Lives of the Poets,* the *English Men of Letters* series). In recent times groups of lives of famous families (e.g., the Rothschilds, the Rockefellers) have been popular. See **biographical anthology, biographical dictionary, brief lives, group biography, multibiography, parallel lives, prosopography, representative, worthies.**

commendatory biography. Eulogistic life, though perhaps more suggestive of the biography of a living person; eulogy being often associated with funerary celebrations; a life of praise. See **eulogy, hagiography.**

commissioned biography. A life, not simply authorized, but assigned by a family, institution, or group, with the suggestion that it is being financially supported; a professional biographer, or ghostwriter, is often commissioned by nonwriters to supply an "official" life. Note the biographer William Novak, whose career so far has included Lee Iococca (1984), the Mayflower Madam (1986), Tip O'Neill (1987), and Oliver North (1991). See **authorized biography.**

commonplace book. A book in which collections of quotations are gathered, often entire poems, short essays, and the like, by an individual in his or her own hand. Johnson defines the term as "a book in which things to be remembered are ranged under general heads." In biography the commonplace book, especially for the period from the seventeenth century through the nineteenth century, may be an important source for information, including not only quotations from others and clippings pasted in, but also personal reflections, comments on readings, literary exercises, pen or pencil sketches, early drafts of letters or literary works.

compendia. Bringing together concise, factual accounts of various persons, perhaps in alphabetical order, though some other logical sequence is possible. See **collective lives.**

composite biography. An infrequently used term that means essentially the same as **prosopography,** or a group of lives of persons in the same field (e.g., *Victorian Visionaries,* lives of early Christian socialists; Leon Edel's *A House of Lions,* on the Bloomsbury Group). See **multibiography, prosopography.**

conduct. Manner of conducting oneself or one's life; behavior; usually with some reference to moral quality, good or bad. Although this term is infrequently used in biographical titles, it may be found in religious autobiography or in military or political memoirs in which, perhaps, a retired general or statesman is justifying his conduct of affairs. Georg Misch (*A History of Autobiography in Antiquity,* Vol. I, p. 25) speaks of "conduct" as a distinct biographical category in antiquity in Egypt; it lacked the unity of the story of a life in the corresponding Greek concept of *bios,* "life."

confessions. See **autobiography, hagiography.**

contextual biography. The part that surrounds a text, i.e., in lifewriting the material outside the direct facts of the life that reveals circumstances in which events occur; places and happenings that surround the life, contributing to the meaning of the text; setting; interconnected parts of the structure of the biography. See **panoramic.**

conversations. Interchange of thoughts and words; familiar discourse or talk; discussion or debate. As early as Eadmer's *Life and Conversations of Anselm* (1124) the biographer used conversation in a life story, adding a more lifelike quality. Dryden in his life of Plutarch, prefatory to the new translation of Plutarch's *Lives* in 1683, also acknowledged the significance of conversation. But the actual words of subjects were seldom used before the eighteenth century, when the conversational element developed strongly, especially through the influence of Boswell, whose most remarkable feature was the preservation of Johnson's talk. Though in some modern lives conversation may be stressed (e.g., George Moore's *Conversations in Ebury Street,* 1924), nothing has ever equaled Boswell. Other classic examples are Martin Luther's *Table Talk* and Goethe's *Conversations With Eckermann.* The tape recorder has made the preservation of talk a phenomenon of modern life-writing. See **dicta, gossip, opinions, oral history, table talk.**

corporate biography. The history of a business or industry, usually based on the founder or major builder of that corporation; e.g., *Iococca* (1984) by William Novak or *Land's Polaroid: A Company and the Man Who Invented It* (1987) by Peter C. Wensburg. See **institutional biography.**

correspondence. Communication by letters; letters contributed to a newspaper or journal. Although the distinction is not always clearly made, letters may mean only those written by one person, whereas correspondence means both sides of the exchange of letters. In the nineteenth century the title "Life and Letters" was often used (Henry Crabb Robinson, *Diary, Reminiscences, and Correspondence,* 1869; John Wilson Croker, *Correspondence and Diaries,* 1884; *The Yale Edition of Horace Walpole's Correspondence,* 1937–1983). See **letters, life and letters.**

counterbiography. A biography that is critical of the conventional, or standard, life of a person, or uses an unusual structure to recount the life. See **doubts, revisionist biography.**

craniology. The study of human skulls and their characteristics; a phase of the eighteenth and nineteenth century enthusiasm for *phrenology;* a means of interpreting character by the shape (the "bumps") of the head. See **phrenology.**

criminal lives. A category of biography, often gathered into collections (e.g., *The Newgate Calendar*), especially popular in the early eighteenth century, when one of the major writers of criminal lives was Daniel Defoe (on Jack Sheppard, Jonathan Wild, etc.). This sub-literary genre has always had a popular appeal, whether through chapbooks, collected lives, or in the twentieth century in films and in ghostwritten autobiographies of bank robbers and long-term prisoners. One of the most widely known was Capt. Alexander Smith's *A*

Complete History of the Lives and Robberies of the Most Notorious Highwaymen, Footpads, Shoplifts, & Cheats of Both Sexes, Wherein their most Secret and Barbarous Murders, Unparalleled Robberies, Notorious Thefts, and Unheard-of Cheats are set in a true light and exposed to Public View, for the Common Benefit of Mankind, which was first published in 1714 and became so popular that it reached a fifth edition (with added volumes) by 1719.

critical biography. The popular meaning of "critical" implies adverse response and some biographies can, of course, be so called, but "critical" in literary lives usually refers to an analytic approach to the subject's published works. Some books on writers are much more, if not entirely, literary criticism rather than biography. See **literary biography.**

critiography. Analogous to "historiography," the study of criticism; a study of texts in history, in the words of Peter Widdowson in his *Hardy in History: A Study in Literary Sociology,* "a study of the process by which 'literature' becomes 'Literature' (just as historiography studies the process by which 'the past' becomes 'History')."

D

death. The "life and death" title of a biography suggests a particular frame for the treatment of a life with emphasis on the death of the subject. This type of life characterized earlier times, through the seventeenth century, when "holy dying" was an influential concept. "Death-bed" scenes in life-writing have always been important ones (e.g., George Cavendish, *The Life and Death of Cardinal Wolsey;* Gilbert Burnet, *Some Passages in the Life and Death of John, Earl of Rochester;* the death of Florence Nightingale in Lytton Strachey's *Eminent Victorians*). The current emphasis on dying, suicide, and death is reflected in life-writing (e.g., John Gunther, *Death Be Not Proud;* Doris Lund, *Eric;* Lynn Caine, *Widow;* Geoffrey Wolff, *Black Sun: The Brief Transit and Violent Eclipse of Harry Crosby;* and several biographical accounts of Sylvia Plath, especially the one by A. Alvarez). See **dialogues of the dead.**

debunking biography. The word debunk, an American colloquialism, means to expose the falseness, to ridicule the sham or exaggerated claims of someone. The term came to be used about the "new" biographies in the 1920s and 1930s, especially after Lytton Strachey's *Eminent Victorians* (1918). The followers of Strachey, the unscholarly idol-smashers writing what they called the "True Life" of a well-known public or literary figure gave biography a bad name. These debunkers tried to knock heroes off pedestals or muddy their character with often ill-founded, if not clearly false, scandalous incidents. They frequently misused "psychological" approaches in order to "interpret" the lives of great men and women. See **hero, vituperative biography.**

deconstruction. A linguistic and philosophical critical approach to literature, as applied to biography. Based on the work of Jacques Derrida and his followers, and originally deriving from the linguistic studies of Ferdinand de Saussure and others, deconstruction, coming from France, has become popular in America (see M. H. Abrams, *A Glossary of Literary Terms,* 1988). It is concerned with the fictionality of any account of a life and the necessary destabilizing of meaning generated by language. Deconstruction's close reading of a text involves its rhetoricity, and stresses the decentered and multiple, the ambiguity of the text. An example of its application to biography is to be found in William H. Epstein's *Recognizing Biography* (1987), particularly in his analysis of Lytton Strachey's *Eminent Victorians.* Deconstruction calls into question the positivistic unity of a life and suggests the impossibility of a definitive life of any subject. See **modernism, postmodernism.**

deductive. See **inductive.**

definitive. See **life.**

detective biography. All biographical works involve a degree of detective work, but some special studies of a biographical nature more clearly come under this term, such as Frederick A. Pottle's *Pride and Negligence: The History of the Boswell Papers* (1982), involving history, life-writing, mystery, and extensive legal proceedings. A. J. A. Symons's *Quest for Corvo* (1934) is another, rather different, but successful example of this type. See **quest.**

diachronic. From Saussurian linguistics, a term used by Frederick Pottle and others for biographical works, meaning in the order of time, chronological; as opposed to *synchronic,* meaning thematic, or simultaneous time. Much less often used is the parallel term *achronic,* meaning without any particular order, as in some memoirs. See William H. Epstein, *Recognizing Biography* (1987). See **chronology.**

dialogues of the dead. A genre established by Lucian, second century Greek rhetorician, presenting conversations of "shades" in Hades, or the underworld; no narrative is involved, but the dead are overheard in conversation; derived in part from the genre *dialogue,* a literary use of dialectic, a form that investigates a subject from two or more points of view. Speakers in dialogues of the dead are usually famous persons from history or from legend. A related form is *imaginary conversations,* such as those by Walter Savage Landor in the 1820s. Writers of dialogues use parallels in the biographies of famous men; often satiric, this form was popular in the eighteenth century; now rare. (See F. M. Keener, *English Dialogues of the Dead: A Critical History, An Anthology, and a Check List,* 1973).

diary. A daily record of events or transactions, a journal; a daily record of matters affecting the writer personally, or that come under his personal observation. Diaries written without plans for publication became a favorite literary activity in the seventeenth century, partly as a result of French influence; many of these actually appeared in published form in the nineteenth century. Many diaries have been published in the nineteenth and twentieth centuries, but the growing awareness of the possibility of publication tends to rob them of the absolute frankness found in Samuel Pepys' *Diary,* kept in code from 1660 to 1669, but not deciphered until 1825 and not completely published in an unexpurgated edition until the 1970s. The term **journal** is generally synonymous with *diary,* but it is often used to cover events of a limited period of time (e.g., Boswell's *Journal of a Tour to the Hebrides,* 1785); it may imply something more elaborate than a diary or more irregular. Terms like *journal-book* or *day-book* are not very common. Since the discovery of the private papers of James Boswell in the 1920s and the continuing publication of volumes of those Boswellian archives by Yale University and McGraw-Hill from the 1950s, the word **journal** has become even more strongly associated with Boswell, whose journal-keeping was a lifelong activity. See the various books on diaries by Arthur Ponsonby; Robert Fothergill's *Private Chronicles* (1974); Steven Kagle's *American Diary Literature* (1979); and the bibliographies by William Matthews.

dicta. Authoritative pronouncements; collections of sayings; plural of *dictum.* The phrase *obiter dictum* (L. "said in passing"), though sometimes used as a title of collected quotations, suggests noteworthy sayings by some person of stature. See **bon mot, conversations.**

dictionary. See **biographical dictionary.**

discography. A systematic listing of phonograph records, tapes, or CDs; a catalogue or comprehensive list of the recordings made by a particular performer or of a composer's works; comparable to a bibliography of a writer's works, includes titles, composers, performances, dates and places of issue; part of the documentation in biographical works on musicians, composers, poets, and other performers.

discovery. A general term, usually applied to the lives of explorers, adventurers, and the like. The term may be used in the sense of new revelations concerning a previously well-known biographical subject.

In Johnson's *Dictionary,* "finding something hidden or secret." In British legal parlance *(Oxford English Dictionary),* "disclosure by a party to an action at the instance of the other party, of facts or documents necessary to maintain his own title."

docudrama. A television term for a historical or biographical program based on documentary film, organized as a dramatic presentation, sometimes called "actuality drama." Although docudramas appear to be factual, they may involve considerable fiction, and they continue to be the subject of controversy. Alex Haley called *Roots* "faction," a blending of fact and fiction, but felt that this distinction was not made clear in the television version. See **cinematic.**

documentation. The preparation and use of evidence and authorities. Scholarly biographies are especially concerned with documentation, including verification of source material through footnotes, bibliographies, and correspondence; well-documented biography uses, where possible, original sources and indicates clearly what those sources are and evaluates the dependability of the materials used. Although the tradition of biographical scholarship is as old as Plutarch, and although Boswell himself documents his account of Johnson by frequent references to authorities (mainly Johnson himself), it is in the twentieth century that scholarly documentation has achieved its heights (e.g., Amy Lowell, *Keats,* 1925; John Nicolay and John Hay, *Abraham Lincoln,* 10 vols., 1890; Leslie Marchand, *Byron,* 3 vols., 1957; Leon Edel, *Henry James,* 5 vols., 1953–1972). See **scholarly biography.**

doubts. An infrequently used term in life-writing, such as in Horace Walpole's *Historic Doubts on Richard III* (1768), suggesting the uncertainty of traditional, or received, or generally accepted views of an historic figure. See **counterbiography, revisionist biography, vituperative biography.**

dual autobiography. An unusual double autobiography, such as "one" by a husband and wife together; dual biography is much more common.

dual biography. The lives of two persons who are closely related, such as husband and wife, father and son, lifelong friends, mother and daughter; to be distinguished from **parallel lives,** in which there is a relationship only of analogous careers or similar historical position of importance. Examples include two sisters, in Jane Dunn's *A Very Close Conspiracy: Vanessa Bell and Virginia Woolf* (1990) and husband and wife, in Lee Hall's portrait of the de Koonings, *Elaine and Bill* (1993), and John Heidenry's *Theirs Was the Kingdom: Lila and DeWitt Wallace and the Story of the Reader's Digest* (1993). See **parallel lives.**

duplex autobiography. The self as a psychological concept and the self as an experienced fact; an example of the application of this metaphorical idea to autobiography is "Gibbon's Memoirs and Their Origins," by John H. Pearson (*Biography* 14, no. 3, Summer 1991). See James Olney, *Metaphors of Self* (1971), p. 39. See **simplex autobiography.**

E

eccentrics. Any persons whose conduct or manners are irregular, odd, or whimsical. The British have always been noteworthy for producing eccentrics, even including such distinguished persons as Samuel Johnson, Thomas Carlyle, George Bernard Shaw, or Oscar Wilde, whose eccentricities are often better known than their great virtues. Often the term is reserved for lesser known figures, like Charles Waterton, Richard Dadd (though here eccentricity goes into madness), and the Sitwells. *Foibles,* or small failings of a biographical subject, may form an important part of the objective picture of a subject. Roger North and Samuel Johnson both insisted on revealing faults in a character. See **character, humors.**

elegiac memoirs. This combined form of elegy and memoir has been referred to by Christopher Ricks in a review as a "very difficult form, but a much-valued one just now [1975]; it is as if the dissolution of other pieties (family ones, religious ones, institutional ones, marital ones) has left an honourable hunger for those publicly attested fidelities which friendship can still incarnate." The term is more acceptable for modern memoirists than "funeral sermon" or "saint's life," but it hardly seems likely that the nineteenth century encomium will return as a major form, even though elegiac memoirs will always be with us. See **elegy.**

elegy. Although this word usually refers to poetry, funeral song, or lamentation for the dead, there are biographical works, usually of the brief, obituary type, that may be called elegies (e.g., Sir Fulke Greville, *Life of the Renowned Sir Philip Sidney*). The impulse to eulogize was evident in the encomium as written in ancient Greece (see Arnoldo Momigliano, *The Development of Greek Biography,* 1971, p. 82). The desire to commemorate the dead probably constitutes the origin of the biographical impulse. See **elegiac memoirs, éloge, epitaph.**

éloge. (From *elogium,* a short saying, or inscription). An expression of praise or commendation; an encomium; a funeral oration; a discourse in honor of a deceased person, e.g., that pronounced by a newly elected member of the French Academy upon his predecessor; a brief summary of a person's character; a biographical notice (usually of a deceased person). Lytton Strachey in the preface to *Eminent Victorians* (1918) complains that the English have no works comparable to the traditional French éloges of writers like Fontenelle and Condorcet.

enacted biography. A term, invented by Ernest Kris in *Psychoanalytic Explorations in Art* (1952), by which is meant the moral influence lives of great persons have upon the actions of readers; the influence upon human lives by biographical models, an idea that is to be found as early as Plutarch and is expanded by Samuel Johnson in *Rambler* No. 60, where he emphasizes the moral value of biography.

epitaph. Strictly speaking, an inscription on a tomb, but the word came to mean any written piece for that memorial purpose. In the late sixteenth century the long, stylized biographical epitaph was very popular (e.g., those written by George Whetstone). Samuel Johnson, an admirer of biography, showed his interest in epitaphs in his life of Pope: "An epitaph may be composed in verse or prose. It is indeed commonly panegyrical; because we are seldom distinguished with a stone but by our friends; but it has no rule to restrain or mollify it, except this, that it ought not to be longer than common beholders may be expected to have leisure and patience to peruse." See **elegiac memoirs, elegy, éloge.**

essay. Although the term was introduced by Montaigne [*essai*] in 1580 and into English by Francis Bacon in 1597, meaning a composition in prose of moderate length on any particular subject, or branch of a subject, in its later application to biographical works it suggested an easy or cursory handling of a life story, limited to a few aspects of a life and abandoning the narrative, or chronological, approach (e.g., Arthur Murphy, *Essay on the Life and Genius of Samuel Johnson,* 1792; Sir William Osler, *An Alabama Student and Other Biographical Essays,* 1908; Conrad Aiken, *Ushant: an Essay,* 1952). See **personal essay.**

estate. The term has the general meaning of class, order, rank in a community or nation; status, standing, position, degree of rank or dignity; in relation to life-writing it means a brief sketch that portrays the conditions of the life more than the individual personality. The term relates to the seventeenth century "character" and was popular in that same period (e.g., Thomas Fuller, *The Holy State and the Profane State,* 1642). See **character.**

ethnobiography. Ethnology (the science of dividing humanity into races and studying their origins, distribution, and characteristics) intersecting with biography to portray a subject in time, within such contexts as linguistic, social, historical, professional, or familial. Most evident in lives of primitives, such as Native Americans, Africans, or Polynesians. See James Clifford, " 'Hanging Up Looking Glasses at

Odd Corners:' Ethnobiographical Prospects," in David Aaron's *Studies in Biography* (1978).

eulogy. A set oration of commendation and praise in honor of a deceased person. Early life-writing is heavily eulogistic, giving unqualified praise to the saint, the monarch, the churchman. Later biographies, too, especially intimate family lives of husbands by wives, of fathers by children, are persistently laudatory. The eighteenth century tended to break away from eulogy (Roger North recommended including "scars and blemishes" even when writing of his own brothers), but the nineteenth century returned to eulogistic life-writing, with rare exceptions. Reticent Victorian biographies confined themselves largely to praise—or silence, as in John Forster's *Life of Dickens*, which failed to note his relationship with Ellen Ternan. The commemorative instinct in life-writing has always been strong, and eulogy is the natural response. See **elegiac memoirs, elegy, éloge, epitaph, widow biography.**

exemplary biography. Lives written with the didactic purpose of serving as models for others, particularly for young people. See **representative.**

exemplum. A moral example or parable, often used in sermons and popular in medieval literature; frequently the subject matter is based on a life situation, an incident or a human relationship. See **fall, hagiography, sermon.**

experimental life-writing. In the history of life-writing many experiments have been tried, some so successful as to establish new techniques (e.g., Plutarch's parallel lives, Rousseau's self-analysis, Conyers Middleton's use of letters, Samuel Johnson's combining biography and criticism, Boswell's use of conversation; in modern times A. J. A. Symons's *Quest for Corvo,* Virginia Woolf's tour de force *Orlando,* Gertrude Stein's *Autobiography of Alice B. Toklas*). In the twentieth century there has been a great deal of experimentation in life-writing, from Edmund Gosse's *Father and Son* (1907), through Lytton Strachey's works, André Maurois's *Ariel,* Gamaliel Bradford's psychographs, Edwin Muir's use of dreams in his autobiography, to John Updike's poetic *Midpoint.* Especially in autobiographical drama, film, and television, experiment has been even more in evidence (e.g., Eugene O'Neill's *Long Day's Journey Into Night,* Peter Ustinov's *Photo Finish,* the films of Federico Fellini and Peter Greenaway).

explication de texte. Close reading and interpretation of the words of a text, more frequently applied to poetry and fiction than to life-writing; originally associated with French schools and their literary training.

exploration. See **travels.**

F

face reading. Interpretation of character or personality by "reading" the face, originally developed by John Kaspar Lavater in the eighteenth century, becoming highly popular in the nineteenth century and developing into **phrenology.** See **physiognomy.**

facthood. Since facts are the basic material of any life story, the addition of the suffix *-hood* suggests a state or condition of facts (as in falsehood) and implies a biography or autobiography that is merely a compilation of facts. See **facticity, factoid.**

facticity. Emphasis on mere facts in life-writing; stress on factual material; a term which came into use in the literature of deconstruction. The relationship of fact to truth is more complex than has generally been recognized. The problem of determining the facts in biography has been a major concern from the beginning, but in modern times the nature of facthood has been the subject of such theorists as William H. Epstein (*Recognizing Biography,* 1987). See **facthood, factoid.**

factoid. A pejorative term coined by Norman Mailer (*Marilyn,* 1973); refers to Maurice Zolotow's biography of Marilyn Monroe as "a book which has fewer facts than factoids... that is, facts which have no existence before appearing in a magazine or newspaper, creations which are not so much lies as a product to manipulate emotions." In downplaying facts (historical facts) in Monroe's life Mailer seems to be rationalizing his own fictive approach to life-writing.

fake lives, or **fictional biography.** The most notorious examples of lives of nonexistent persons, written with the intent to deceive, are found in **biographical dictionaries.** See "Appleton's Spurious Articles," by John Blythe Dobson (*Biography* 16, no. 4, Fall 1993). Unlike **mock biography** or **parody biography,** which are obvious literary ventures and are so understood by the intelligent reader, fake lives are devious attempts to make money by avoiding any laborious research. The identification of such forgers is even more difficult than the task of revealing their corrupt work.

fall. A frequent motif of early English biography is that of the **Wheel of Fortune,** the rise to success and the subsequent fall to ruin, destruction, and death. A fall may suggest a succumbing to temptation, a lapse into sin or folly, and the account may well be didactic, part of a sermon, a homily, or an exemplum. As a Christian religious concept it is, of course, related to the Fall of Man, as seen in the story of the Garden of Eden and Adam and Eve. (E.g., John Lydgate, *The Falls of*

Princes, based on Boccaccio's *De Casibus Virorum Illustrium,* four-
teenth- and fifteenth-century poetic works; George Cavendish, *The
Life and Death of Cardinal Wolsey,* 1557.) See **exemplum, sermon.**

family history. Related to genealogy and to biographies of two or more
family members, as in father and son or mother and daughter lives.
Some outstanding biographies of families have been done in the field
of royal history, as of the Romanovs, or of wealthy business or indus-
trial families, such as the Rockefellers. Examples of more domestic
family tales are Louise Hall Tharp's *The Peabody Sisters of Salem*
(1950), Catherine Drinker Bowen's *Family Portrait* (1970), Jonathan
Yardley's *Our Kind of People* (1989), and R. W. B. Lewis's *The Jameses:
A Family Narrative* (1991).

feminist life-writing. Although the cultural phenomenon of feminism
is manifested notably in the late twentieth century, one can find evi-
dences of it as early as Chaucer and Margery Kempe and in the late
seventeenth century in Margaret Lucas and Lucy Hutchinson.
Certainly by the late eighteenth century and Mary Wollstonecraft
(even including William Godwin), feminism was flourishing.
However, it is in the late twentieth century that the lives of women,
by women, for women and men, became a major phase of contemporary literature. Not surprisingly autobiographies and diaries consti-
tute the earliest examples of feminism in life-writing. The essential
feature of truly *feminist* lives is the emphasis on what makes a woman's
life characteristically female as opposed to male, no matter how much
an individual life may involve relationships with the opposite sex.
Among many examples Virginia Woolf is an effective illustration, not
only for her extensive and widely known diary, but also for her two
expressly "feminist" books *A Room of One's Own* (1929) and *Three
Guineas* (1938). In more recent years the books written about Virginia
Woolf reflect the varying types of feminism in life-writing. Louise
DeSalvo's *Virginia Woolf: The Impact of Childhood Sexual Abuse on Her
Life and Work* (1990) represents controversially extreme views by an
author who is known as a feminist (she is also the author of *Nathaniel
Hawthorne: A Feminist Reading*). On the other hand, Jane Dunn's *A
Very Close Conspiracy: Vanessa Bell and Virginia Woolf* (1990) is a penetrating and subtle biographical study of two remarkable sisters, both
of whom would certainly be called feminists. Diary writing (and publication) has increased widely since Anaïs Nin and Virginia Woolf, and
such self-revelation is the seedbed of feminism. See **lesbian life-
writing.**

flashback. The technique in fiction, also possible though infrequent in
life-writing, of interrupting the chronological progression to present
material from an earlier time before returning to the regular time
sequence. *Flashforward* is a less frequently used device.

furor biographicus. A term used by Freud showing his awareness of the growing popularity of biography during the years of his publication of case histories; his own biographical works are limited to two: *Leonardo: A Study in Psychosexuality* (1910), and with William C. Bullitt on Woodrow Wilson (written in the 1930s but published in 1967).

G

gay life-writing. An ever increasing category in biography and especially in autobiography, from coming-out-of-the-closet and sensational lives to serious defense of an accepted way of life; in tone, from grim to joyous, from tortured to celebratory. Although the term "gay" is relatively modern, early awareness and concern for homosexuality in the twentieth century is to be found in Oscar Wilde's *De Profundis* (1905, though not fully published until 1964), and in biographical works associated with Aubrey Beardsley, André Gide, Marcel Proust, Walt Whitman, Tchaikovsky, and other well-known figures. But it is only in recent years, from the 1970s, that openness has flourished (see John D'Emilio, *Making Trouble: Essays on Gay History, Politics, and the University,* 1992). There are differences between male homosexual accounts and lesbian lives. As D'Emilio points out: "In gay experience sexual attraction usually precedes a deeper relationship. In Lesbian experience it is more likely that sexual activity follows an already established intimacy." Biographers of members of the Bloomsbury Group have long been involved in dealing with nontraditional sexual experience, which varies according to the subject as well as the life-writer. The rise of feminism, the easing of censorship, and the Gay Liberation movement have assisted in the growth of gay life-writing. Representative subjects have included Baron Corvo, J. R. Ackerley, Christopher Isherwood, E. M. Forster, James Baldwin, John Cheever, Roy Cohn, the Cambridge spies (Maclean, Philby, Burgess, Blunt), T. E. Lawrence, Somerset Maugham, and scores of others. Related topics include transsexuals (e.g., Jan Morris, *Conundrum,* 1974), bisexuality, transvestism (J. Edgar Hoover), and AIDS, which though often associated with gays is not restricted to homosexuals. See **lesbian life-writing.**

genealogy. An account of one's descent from an ancestor or ancestors by the enumeration of the intermediate persons; a pedigree. Genealogical studies have been associated with life-writing since earliest times. In scholarly biography it is usual to have genealogical charts indicating descent; this is especially true of the lives of royalty or nobility, but it may also be used where there are complex family relationships and important collateral figures in a life story (e.g., the "Family Tree" at the beginning of Quentin Bell's *Virginia Woolf*, 1972). For a structural definition of genealogy, see the work of Michel Foucault (e.g., "Nietzsche, Genealogy, History," 1971). See **family history.**

genius. Extraordinary power of mind, often revealed by great success in art, invention, politics, the military, or many another field. The word has frequently been misused, but it was popular in the late nineteenth and early twentieth centuries for lives called Men of Genius, or Man of Genius, so that the term has tended to lose its real usefulness.

ghostwriting. Writing by a person who poses as the author; often found in political, popular, and "Hollywood" biographies; in earlier days the ghostwriter's name was often lacking; today, in an attempt at greater honesty, the ghostwriter's name often appears as "in collaboration with" or "as told to." See **commissioned biography.**

Gospels. Literally, "good news," but specifically referring to the first four books of the New Testament, giving the story of Christ's life and teachings in the versions by Matthew, Mark, Luke, and John. The term sometimes refers to the body of doctrine taught by Jesus and his Apostles. Down through the ages there have been more biographies of Jesus Christ than of any other person, with the possible exception of Napoleon; but all lives of Christ are dependent upon the four Gospels. In general terms "gospel" may refer to any revelation from heaven. See **hagiography.**

gossip. Idle talk, usually spontaneous chatter between friends or among small groups, about people. It can contribute to life-writing in various ways, the most notable example being Boswell's *Life of Johnson*. Gossip may be harmless or malicious, innocuous or scandalous, frivolous or destructive. Both private and public, gossip may reveal the character of both the subject and the speaker. One of Johnson's definitions of the term: "One who runs about tattling like women at a lying-in." A thorough literary analysis may be found in Patricia M. Spack's *Gossip* (1985). See **-ana, scandal.**

graffiti. Plural of *graffito*, an archeological term for drawing or writing scratched on a wall. Although this term is not directly concerned with life-writing, the words and phrases written on walls in public places are often autobiographical in nature ("Kilroy was here"), and in their expressiveness often reveal a personality, however brilliant or retarded. Graffiti have been a subject for serious study by historians.

grangerize. To extra-illustrate a book, with drawings, prints, engravings, newspaper clippings, and the like; to mutilate a book by clipping out its illustrations for such use. The name derives from James Granger (1723–1776), English biographer, who in 1769 published his *Biographical History of England* to be thus illustrated.

group biography. Although the general definition of "a collection of lives with some thematic basis" has been used, new discoveries in life-writing stress the communal over the individual, so that Margot Peters, in "Group Biography: Challenges and Methods" (in Anthony Friedson's *New Directions in Biography*, 1981) defines it as "the interweaving of a number of lives by one writer to show how they interact with each other." Group biography now may be related to group therapy, encounter groups, role-playing groups, and the like. Modern examples include Norman and Jeanne MacKenzie's *The Fabians,* Leon Edel's *Bloomsbury: A House of Lions,* James R. Mellow's *Charmed Circle: Gertrude Stein and Company,* and Janet McCalman's *Journeyings: The Biography of a Middle-Class Generation, 1920–1990.* See **collective lives, group portrait, multibiography, parallel lives, prosopography.**

group portrait. As in painting, where some family groups (e.g., Thomas More's by Holbein) or clubs and the like (as in photography) are treated together, so in life-writing several persons, usually in a related association, may be done together. See **collective lives, group biography, multibiography, parallel lives, prosopography.**

H

hackiography. Derogatory term for the "mostly warts" biography—the "wartrait" as used in *Vanity Fair,* in commentary on the biographies by Kitty Kelley (Frank Sinatra, Nancy Reagan, et al.). The word is a play on **hagiography.**

hagiography. Saints' lives as a branch of literature or legend, generally applied to collections of biographies of saints and to other sacred writings. Early saints' lives were arranged by the calendar, a chronological or numerical listing of the fete days or the days for celebration of the mass in honor of a particular saint. **Acta sanctorum,** or records of passions, trials, martyrdoms, miracles associated with the saints; the term is generally applied to all the saints, the "communion of saints" (see Charles W. Jones, *Saints' Lives and Chronicles in Early England,* 1947), or the "life of the saints," which indicates why there is no concern with differentiation of the life of an individual saint from all others: all saints are one in God; whatever is characteristic of one saint is characteristic of all. The acts of the saints were often collected in a *martyrology*, a register or list of martyrs in order of their commemoration; in antiquity, the **necrology** of a religious house. These registers would note the place, date, and sufferings of their deaths. Saints' lives are so generalized as to be meaningless in the modern view of what biography should be; however, some of the earliest saints' lives in England (written in Latin) are more individualized than the later lives of saints (e.g., Adamnan's *St. Columba*, c. 692; Bede's *St. Cuthbert*, c. 731). Later lives became more generalized, especially after they were written in English. A good reference book, with an informative introduction, is Donald Attwater, *The Penguin Dictionary of Saints* (1965), containing in alphabetical order accounts of 750 saints (out of more than 10,000 saints on record). See also J. F. Webb, *Lives of the Saints* (1965), which includes lives of St. Brendan, St. Cuthbert, and St. Wilfrid; note also *The Golden Legend*, a thirteenth century collection of saints' lives by Jacopo da Voragine. See the article on "hagiography" in the *Catholic Encyclopedia*, which divides hagiography into two types, practical and critical.

hands. Although biographers have shown more concern with their subject's facial features, hands are also significant, especially in portraiture; but one should note that the hands in painted portraits through the eighteenth century are not necessarily those of the sitter (a notable exception is Sir Joshua Reynolds' profile of Johnson, without a wig and with expressive upheld hands, about 1769). In the nineteenth and twentieth centuries biographers have sometimes used illustrations of plaster casts of subjects' hands. Queen Victoria was concerned to display the model hands, in marble, of her numerous infants. Hands can be used to reveal aspects of character; Renoir said that he always judged people for the first time by their hands. The word "hands" can also signify handwriting, as in Anthony G. Petti, *English Literary Hands from Chaucer to Dryden* (1977). See Jonathan Goldberg, *Writing Matter, From the Hands of the English Renaissance* (1990). See **handwriting analysis.**

handwriting analysis. The study of handwriting, or graphology, as a means of interpreting character has long been known, but only in recent years have psychologists seriously undertaken the analysis of handwriting, or "brainwriting" as it might be called, for the understanding of certain character traits. This approach has not been widely used in life-writing, but it seems likely to become more important in the future. (See John A. Garraty, *The Nature of Biography*, 1970, where he discusses the subject under the topic of "The Problem of Personality.") In some biographical works even a person's "doodles" have been used for character analysis. A new technique for deciphering handwriting characteristics by computer is called "graphometry."

hero. The concept of the person who is admired for great achievements, for noble qualities, for bravery, firmness, enterprise, accomplishments, is one that has predominated from ancient times to the present, although certain periods have been better known than others for bringing forth heroes. Hero-worship, or the adulation of great individuals, may well be considered antipathetic to the biographical impulse—"No man is a hero to his valet"—but this is not necessarily so. Most great biographies have been at least sympathetic studies by admirers, if not hero-worshipping encomiums. The great ages of heroes—antiquity, the Renaissance, the Romantic Age—produced heroic lives (Alexander the Great, Michelangelo, Byron) and the biographies written of these heroes, in any age, tend to reflect hero-worship. Perhaps the best examination of this attitude toward both history and life-writing is that of Thomas Carlyle in *On Heroes, Hero-Worship and the Heroic in History* (1841). In the modern age, which seems to be one that does not produce heroes, perhaps the *antihero* is more representative, though it is much easier to find the antihero in fiction than in biography. It may be that the characteristic antiheroes of modern life-writing are more frequently found in autobiography. The modern debunking life is a kind of reversal of the hero-worshipping life. See also Joseph Campbell, *The Hero with a Thousand Faces* (1956). See **debunking, valet biography.**

heterobiography. Biography written by another person; opposite to **autobiography.** An infrequently used term.

historiette. A short history, or story based on fact; an anecdote. Though this term was used in the early eighteenth century by both Thomas Brown and Roger North and later in the century by Madame D'Arblay, it has been rarely used. The *Oxford English Dictionary* gives *historietto* as an alternative version for this term. See **anecdote.**

historiography. The principle or methodology of writing history; the art of writing history; more exactly, the study of the writing of history. See **history, oral history.**

historiometry. The use of quantitative analysis of data about individuals to study human behavior in general. Especially useful in studying such phenomena as genius, creativity, leadership, and aggression. See Dean Keith Simonton, *Psychology, Science, and History: An Introduction to Historiometry* (1991).

history. Although the term now generally indicates an account of events affecting communities and nations, or the events themselves, in earlier times it was used to describe the facts of individual lives, which we now classify as **biography.** Not until the end of the seventeenth century was biography clearly distinguished from history, although the distinction is made as early as Plutarch. Even as late as the nineteenth century the distinguished historian-biographer Thomas Carlyle made much of the interrelations of the two genres, saying that "History is the essence of innumerable Biographies." Modern historians would not hold to this view. According to Arthur Marwick (*The Nature of History*, 1971), there are three levels for the meaning of history: (1) "the entire human past," (2) "man's attempt to describe and interpret that past," and (3) "history as a discipline" or subject for systematic study. Such forms as the **memoir** and the **"life-and-times"** biography are not always clearly to be distinguished from history. See **biography, memoir.**

holograph. Wholly written by the person in whose name it appears, as a holograph letter, all in the handwriting of the person who composed and signed the letter. Although the term is usually applied to letters, it may also be used about manuscripts of various kinds and is especially important in relation to letters, wills, and other documentary evidence.

humors. In the Middle Ages the physiological theory of the four humors was that the body was made up of four fluids: blood, phlegm, yellow bile, and black bile (derived from the four elements: air, water, fire, and earth). The predominance of any one humor determined the characteristic temperament of a person: sanguine, phlegmatic, choleric, melancholic. Disease was a result of the vapors sent off by a predominance of one or more humors. Many examples may be found in Shakespeare and in Ben Jonson's comedies. These concepts, which also affected life-writing, begin to disappear in the eighteenth century and are replaced by new theories of human character, especially by the time of the twentieth century when psychology gave us the extrovert instead of the sanguine person, or the introvert instead of the melancholy individual, and so on. Among Samuel Johnson's nine variant definitions of "humour" is "general turn of temper or mind." See **character, character sketch.**

hysterians. Robert Scholes's term for "new journalism" writers like Tom Wolfe and Norman Mailer, since they record the hysteria of contemporary life.

I

iconography. In general terms this word refers to the branch of knowledge that deals with the representation of persons or objects by any application of the arts of design; any book or work in which this is done; the description or illustration of any subject by means of drawings or figures. *Iconology,* a related term, deals with symbolical representation or symbolism. The word is as old as the seventeenth century, but in modern times it has come to be much more widely, yet also much more specifically, used. In life-writing iconography refers to the images of the subject—portraits, sketches, photographs, and the like. The use of illustration in biography is as old as the Middle Ages, where chronicles of kings were illustrated by woodcuts of crowned heads (sometimes repeated over and over again, showing that characteristically in that age there was little differentiation among kings). By the Renaissance the highly individualized portraits (e.g., Holbein's Henry VIII, or his Thomas More or Erasmus) parallel the highly individualized life stories. Most characteristic for many years was—and is—the frontispiece portrait in a biography; some collections of the portraits of major figures (e.g., Abraham Lincoln, Alexander Pope, William Wordsworth) have been published separately. At least one publishing house (Thames and Hudson, London) has specialized in illustrated biographies that include not only portraits and photographs of the subject of the life, but also illustrations of related figures, of places, of title pages of books, and of manuscripts. Close analytical study of all existing portraits or photographs of a subject as a means of understanding character has not yet often been done, but rare scholarly works, such as W. K. Wimsatt's *The Portraits of Alexander Pope* (1965), are indispensable to all succeeding biographers of the subject. Some faces, to be sure, are more revealing or more memorable than others. Clive James said that when compiling a photographic file of authors, "you had to be careful with the Bloomsbury bunch because they all looked the same, as in a horse-breeder's catalogue." Nevertheless Elizabeth P. Richardson's *Bloomsbury Iconography* (1989) copes effectively with this problem. See **photoanalysis.**

identity. Oneness; the sameness of a person at all times or in all circumstances; individuality or continuity of personality; personal or individual existence. The concept of identity crisis, or a loss of the sense of personal sameness or continuity, a loss of "ego-identity" in Erikson's phrase, has become widely used as a result of Erik Erikson's work (*Childhood and Society,* 1950; *Young Man Luther,* 1958; *Identity: Youth and Crisis,* 1968). Perhaps contemporary autobiography reveals more concern with identity problems than does contemporary biography, but Erikson's *Luther* is a prototype of this particular psychological approach.

idolatria. Lives written idolizing the subject, even more subservient to the subject than eulogies, epitaphs, or "worthies." Probably most common among saints' lives in medieval times and most common today on figures from moviedom or rock stars.

illustrations. See **iconography.**

inductive. Some commentators on life-writing have divided biographies into two classes: *deductive* and *inductive*. Since deductive means reasoning from the general to the particular, and inductive from the particular to the general, it is evident that the deductive biographer begins with a preconceived notion of the subject and proceeds to compile the facts to illustrate his position, while the inductive biographer, using the scientific method, accumulates the details of factual evidence and presents them in such a way as to allow the readers to form their own opinions about the subject. Obviously both these methods are used by life-writers—used simultaneously, no doubt. Yet the medieval saint's life represents the extreme deductive type, and Boswell's method represents the inductive approach. Clearly the eighteenth century advances in life-writing—as in many other areas— reveal the rise of the scientific, or inductive method. More recent studies of Boswell, however, have stressed the fact that he is really much more deductive than had previously been thought. These terms have some general usefulness, but they cannot easily be rigidly applied as critical terms in life-writing.

institutional biography. Another term for the history of an institution, such as an industry or an academic institution. Ed Regis's *Who Got Einstein's Office* narrates the activities of the Institute of Advanced Study at Princeton as much as the life of Einstein. Sometimes the life of a major figure in business or academia can also be classed under this term. See **corporate biography.**

intellectual biography. Analogous to "intellectual history," which came out of the general term "history of ideas." Emphasis on the education of the subject or the social and historical context of a life, as in Ray Monk's *Wittgenstein* (1990) and Robert Sidelsky's *John Maynard Keynes* (1983, 1993). Even an autobiography, such as that of John Stuart Mill or Henry Adams, can be so classed.

interview. Formal, face-to-face conference with a person to gather information or opinion; personal meeting. Often interviews are published independently and later used as biographical material. Boswell's method was basically that of the interviewer, although conversation suggests more than merely listening to talk by one subject. See **conversations, oral history.**

invention. A fabrication; fictitious statement or story. The term is a derogatory one when applied to either history or life-writing, although welcomed by post-structuralist biographers and used imaginatively in works like Peter Ackroyd's *Dickens* (1990), where he used invented dialogue throughout to highlight elements of Dickens's character.

inverted autobiography. A term invented by Paul-Gabriel Boucé when, in surveying eighteenth and nineteenth century biographies of Tobias Smollett, he finds the novelist the victim of wholesale appropriation of episodes taken from the fictional lives of his heroes (Roderick Random, Peregrine Pickle, etc.) and applied to the life of Smollett himself. See **biographical fallacy.**

J

jest biography. Translation of *Schwankbiographien,* a term used by Ernst Schulz to describe a minor seventeenth century form of anecdotal, fictional lives that, in spirit and in method, are close to jest-books (e.g., *The Life of Long Meg of Westminster,* 1620). See **criminal lives, mock biography, parody biography.**

journal. Daily record of events; logbook. See **diary, log.**

journalistic life-writing. Both biography and autobiography can be "journalistic." The lives of news reporters, photographers, and editors have flourished in the twentieth century because their professions are notably concerned with people, often famous people. Not only are their personal accounts (e.g., John Gunther, James Reston, Charles Kurault, Russell Baker) popular, but some professional biographers began their careers as journalists (e.g., Virginia Cowles). Lives of living political figures are characteristically journalistic in style, as many of the books on the Kennedy family members reveal. Journalistic autobiographies are frequently recognized by their titles, such as Malcolm W. Browne's *Muddy Boots and Red Socks* (1993).

journey. See **tour, travels, voyages.**

juvenilia. Youthful compositions; immature work, literary or artistic (e.g., the early writings of the Brontë children), significant for the biographer's study of childhood and development.

L

"laundry list" biography. Lives written with detailed, factual material; usually a derogatory term, suggesting overemphasis on minor, unimportant facts.

lesbian life-writing. The term "lesbian" for female homosexuality is much older than the term "gay" for male homosexuality. Like the word "Sapphic," it derives from the poet Sappho of the isle of Lesbos (c. 600 B.C.). Although lesbian writers have been known from earliest times, in modern times the "coming out" of lesbian autobiography and biography has been relatively slow until recent decades. First came novels which were thinly disguised autobiographies (e.g., Radclyffe Hall's *The Well of Loneliness*, 1928). In 1933 Gertrude Stein's *The Autobiography of Alice B. Toklas* was a disguise in different fashion. A biography of a lesbian couple appeared in 1971: Elizabeth Mavor's *The Ladies of Llangollen: A Study in Romantic Friendship*, a frank and sensitive account of the elopement of two late eighteenth century young women, who lived together in Wales for the remainder of their lives. The larger proportion of modern lesbian lives are auto-biographies (e.g., Kate Millett, May Sarton), but any biographer today of such subjects as Vita Sackville-West, Sylvia Townsend Warner, Elizabeth Bishop, and many another, including such sports figures as Martina Navratilova, would have to be concerned with the subject's sexual orientation. In *The Tradition of Women's Autobiography* (1986), Estelle C. Jelinek discusses the essential differences between gay and lesbian lives, pointing out that women's narrative mode of free association, with flashbacks and flashforwards, reveals the "fragmentation of women's experience of reality," whereas men's more explicit eroticism is generally presented in chronological order. The rise of feminism in the latter half of the twentieth century has contributed to the increase and frankness of lesbian life-writing. See **feminist life-writing, gay life-writing.**

letters. Written messages. One of the most important forms of biographical material is letters. In earlier times the word *epistle* was used, though this suggests a more formal kind of communication, perhaps addressed to a group (as in the New Testament). In antiquity collected epistles were published (e.g., Pliny, Cicero). An important point in the history of biography was Thomas Sprat's refusal to use private letters in his *Life of Abraham Cowley* (1668); since this was an influential biography, it tended to minimize the use of personal letters in biography until the middle of the next century, when Conyers Middleton, in his *Life of Cicero* (1741), not only used letters extensively, but interwove passages from them into his narrative text. Generally credited with being the first to use letters in a literary biography is William Mason in his *Memoirs of Gray* (1775), which is really little more than a collection of 130 carefully edited letters with short narrative intervals. Boswell in his *Life of Johnson* (1791) adopts Mason's method, introducing over 300 letters. Letters had been used earlier by Izaak Walton in the seventeenth century in his lives (e.g., John Donne, George Herbert) and occasionally by other biographers. Since the eighteenth century, which was a great letter-writing period, the use of letters in lives has become extensive. While the recipient of a letter owns the actual document, the writer or his heirs retain the copyright. See **correspondence.**

lexicography. The art or practice of writing dictionaries. See **biographical dictionary.**

life. The written story of a life; a biography. Used in a title the term *life* suggests a complete survey of a career from birth to death. In various forms (e.g., Life and Letters, Life and Times, Life and Death) it appears in a great number of biographical titles, although the present-day trend is toward a more subtle, novel-like designation (e.g., *The Stricken Deer, The Thistle and the Rose, Son of Woman, Search for a Soul*). There are three modifying adjectives that are frequently used with the word "life:" *official, standard,* and *definitive,* and these should be differentiated as clearly as possible. An **official life** indicates a biography that has been commissioned by some authority—family, friends, some agency, society, or association. For example, the widow of a famous man commissions someone to write the official life of her late husband—and more often than not this leads to trouble (what to include and what to leave out; competition from rival, "unauthorized" biographers; disappointment in the final product). Often subsequent biographies are responses to, supplements of, or even attacks on the official life. The **standard life** of any person is that biography generally recognized as having the greatest degree of excellence and authority when compared with other lives of the same person. With the passing of years, even with the coming of better, more thorough biographies, the earlier standard life may continue to be referred to as the standard life (a life may be both the official and the standard at the same time), but the new, scholarly, detailed, carefully documented life may be classified as the **definitive life.** This term is less exact and is consequently more casually used, but it is a useful designation and is more widely used in the present time than ever before. One difficulty is that, over the years, one "definitive" biography may be replaced by another. John Forster's *Life of Dickens* (1872) could be called both an official and a standard life, but certainly not "definitive"; perhaps Edgar Johnson's two-volume life of Dickens (1952) could be called the definitive life, but that may be an insecure designation. An interesting modern example of a standard life discovered to be virtually autobiography was Florence E. Hardy's *Early Years of Thomas Hardy* (1928) and *Later Years of Thomas Hardy* (1930). Hardy dictated and wrote almost all of the two volumes himself. Perhaps these volumes can still be called the standard, or official, life, but the definitive biography by Michael Millgate (1982) has been supplemented by Millgate's revised edition of Florence Hardy's life, indicating her revisions and omissions from

Hardy's original work. Understandably these terms are not applied to autobiography. More cautious reviewers may refer to lives as "most detailed" rather than "definitive." Such works as Leslie Marchand's *Byron*, Leon Edel's *Henry James*, George D. Painter's *Proust*, and Lawrance Thompson's *Robert Frost* are referred to as "definitive." See **testamentary acts, widow biography.**

life and letters. The characteristic biography of the nineteenth century, multivolume and a kind of funereal monument, radically attacked by Lytton Strachey, was the "life and letters" or the "life and times" biographies of the Victorian Age (e.g., G. O. Trevelyan, *The Life and Letters of Macaulay*, 2 vols. 1876; David Mason, *The Life and Times of John Milton*, 7 vols., 1859–1894). Michael Millgate (*Testamentary Acts*, 1992) points out that John Lockhart's life of his father-in-law, Sir Walter Scott, essentially established the life and letters form. A modern variant is Gillian Fenwick's *Leslie Stephen's Life in Letters: A Bibliographical Study* (1993). See **correspondence, letters, testamentary acts.**

life-writing. In the narrower sense this term means **biography,** but in general it may include **autobiography** as well, so that it is actually a more inclusive term than biography, even though some people may consider the word biography to include autobiographical works, letters, diaries, and the like. *Life-writing* has been used since the eighteenth century, although it has never been as widely current as biography and autobiography since these words came into the language. Some writers may prefer the Anglo-Saxon rooted phrase, life-writing, to those Latin and Greek based words.

literary biography. A descriptive term for the lives of men and women writers. Sometimes it is assumed that a literary biography is concerned more with the life of the mind than it is with action, with the creative process more than events. One of the best modern discussions is Leon Edel's *Literary Biography* (1957). Dennis W. Petrie deals with literary biography (*Ultimately Fiction*, 1981) and quotes Richard Altick's (1965) remark that it is a "quest for the creator behind the creation . . . couched in the language of the art with which they deal," making literary biography almost a subgenre. Even as late as 1978 Justin Kaplan suggests that "a strong case should be made for enlarging the term 'literary biography' to include books that have literary qualities and not necessarily literary subjects." Today the term generally applies to any biography or autobiography with literary qualities, regardless of the professional field of the subject. An example of the use of the term is the title of the multivolume series *American Writers: A Collection of Literary Biographies*, edited by Lea Baechler and A. Walton Litz (1991).

log or **logbook.** The official record of a ship's voyage, including meteorological, nautical, and other information. Although one thinks of the weather and the air or nautical location as being the usual entries in logbooks, they may also include other commentaries relating to the trip or voyage. In the biographies of seamen and airmen, logbooks are important in relation to the facts of specific voyages, and they may be important for additional, more personal, commentary. The terms may be used in a metaphorical sense (e.g., Jay Leyda, *The Melville Log,* 1951). G. K. Hall and Twayne Publishers are undertaking an "American Authors' Logs Series," which will present scholarly chronologies of the lives of major American authors. See **chronology.**

M

marginalia. Marginal notes, often indicative, when found in books read by the subject of a biography, of his immediate reactions to a particular text and possibly of his basic philosophical views or attitudes toward life; a significant source for the life-writer.

martyrology. See **hagiography.**

Marxist biography. Lives of Communist figures generally, but any biography which reflects the view of human life as the product of social and economic conditions, particularly the evil of class or of bourgeois capitalism, as opposed to the revolutionary worker of the proletariat; the philosophy of Marx and Engels, i.e., historical materialism, as evidenced especially in the heroes of the Communist states. Marxist life-writing is generally unfriendly to individual specificity and to such categories as feminism.

mask. A covering for the face, used figuratively in biography to characterize subjects disguising their real personalities; multiple personalities are sometimes referred to as masks; e.g., Brendan Gill's *Many Masks: A Life of Frank Lloyd Wright* (1987) and Richard Ellmann's *Yeats: The Man and the Masks* (1948, 1962). See **persona.**

materials. The constituent parts, the apparatus or tools; in life-writing the evidence available concerning the subject, such as letters, diaries, journals, reminiscences, and the like. In recent years new kinds of materials have become available, such as photographs, motion pictures, and tape recordings, especially for public figures. An example of the use of the term in a title is John Lord Hervey's *Some Materials Toward the Memoirs of the Reign of King George II.* See **oral history.**

mediated biography. A term defined and fully illustrated by Ruth Hoberman (1987). Basing her discussion on Percy Lubbock's and

Henry James's concerns with point of view (the narrator in fiction), she sees the biographer as one whose "perception displaces the subject." Mediated biographers stress the "presence of a perceiver between the subject and the narrative;" they are not so much concerned with chronology or action as with personality or character; not with development, but with pattern or repetition, with "the story of the story." Illustrative mediated biographies are Henry James's *William Wetmore Story and His Friends* (1903) and A. J. A. Symons's *The Quest for Corvo* (1934).

medical biography. Either the life of a physician or the life of any subject from the point of view of medical history; illnesses, hospitalization, the effect of illness upon a family, and the like. Autobiography frequently concerns itself with medical history or illness (e.g., Llewelyn Powys's *Skin For Skin*, 1925). Some physicians have published interesting medical accounts (e.g., George Pickering, *Creative Malady: Illness in the Lives and Minds of Charles Darwin, Florence Nightingale, Mary Baker Eddy, Sigmund Freud, Marcel Proust, Elizabeth Barrett Browning*, 1974; and two books by William B. Ober, *Boswell's Clap and Other Essays: Medical Analyses of Literary Men's Afflictions*, 1979, and *Bottoms Up! A Pathologist's Essays on Medicine and the Humanities*, 1987).

meditation. A written or spoken discourse in which a topic, usually religious, is treated in a meditative manner, or a discourse designed to guide the reader or hearer in devotional reflection.

megabiography. A term invented to describe the massive, many volumed, modern scholarly lives that in recent years have become more frequent again, after the emphasis upon brevity stressed by Lytton Strachey in his 1918 preface to *Eminent Victorians*. Paul M. Kendall, in *The Art of Biography* (1965), classifies eight types of modern lifewriting and among these includes "Behemoth biography" ("not so much for their size but for their mass") and "superbiography," "a twentieth-century biographical phenomenon" which "grandly exploits both the 'literary element' and the 'scientific element'," and he calls Leon Edel's *Henry James* an example of the type. He does not use the word *megabiography*, but it is essentially the same thing. See **omnium-gatherum.**

memoirs. A record of events, not purporting to be a complete history, but treating of such matters as come within the personal knowledge or within the memory of the writer, or are obtained from particular sources of information. The incidents recorded may come from a person's own life or from persons whom he knows or has known; an autobiographical record. The French term *memoire* was brought into England in the early eighteenth century. Memoir ordinarily differs from autobiography in being less formally organized and in centering more upon social and historical background, less upon private life; but memoirs may frequently be gossipy or scandalous in nature (e.g., *Memoirs of Count Grammont,* 1713). Several writers within the Bloomsbury Group had a Memoir Club, which at various meetings listened to the memoirs read by one of its members. The word "memoir" is sometimes used in a subtitle of an autobiography (e.g., Adam Hochschild's *Half the Way Home: A Memoir of Father and Son,* 1986). See **autobiography.**

memorabilia. Memorable or noteworthy things; matters or events worth remembering. The term suggests miscellaneous items associated with reminiscences, memoirs, recollections, autobiography.

memorats. Personal narrative; a term used by folklorists.

memorials. In a limited sense, merely notes or memoranda; more generally, records, chronicles, memoirs, often containing personal reminiscences of the history of a person, place, or event. The term may refer to any brief biographical items calculated to preserve the memory of the subject. In a title the term suggests an attitude of reverence or affection on the part of the writer (e.g., James A. Froude, *Letters and Memorials of Jane Welsh Carlyle,* 1883).

memory. The power or act of remembering; commemoration or remembrance; fame after death; posthumous reputation. Memory, as distinguished from **recollections** or **reminiscences,** may be involuntary; it is nevertheless basic to the autobiographer. One of the major aspects of Boswell's genius was the power of his memory. The plural term, *memories,* is often used in autobiographical titles. See **nostalgia.**

metoscopy. The art of reading character from the forehead or face of an individual; the psychological zone of the face. See **face reading, physiognomy.**

miniature. Although "portraits in miniature" is a phrase often associated with Lytton Strachey, for his small-scale biographical works in the collection so named, before Strachey the short lives by Charles Whibley and Edmund Gosse helped to popularize the form. The *Brief Lives of John Aubrey* and the historiettes by Gédéon Tallemant, both writing in the seventeenth century but "discovered" later, anticipate more modern writers. See Ira B. Nadel's *Biography: Fiction, Fact, and Form,* 1984. See **cameo, historiette, profile.**

mini-memoir. Infrequently used term for very short memoirs; used in a derogatory sense by a reviewer of James Sherry's *Bloomsbury Heritage, Their Mothers and Their Aunts;* Elizabeth F. Boyd wrote: "rather superficial biographical sketches ... one is tempted to call them mini-memoirs because they seem so Victorian."

miscellany. A mixture or medley; a collection of various biographical bits without strict organization or incorporation into a single entity (e.g., G. B. Hill, *Johnsonian Miscellanies,* 1897). Miscellanies may be separate treatises or studies on a subject gathered into one volume. See **-ana, anecdotes.**

mock biography. A counterfeit or imitative life, using biographical methods or techniques, but actually fiction. Many novels are make-believe biographies or autobiographies, as were most early novels (e.g., *Robinson Crusoe, Tom Jones, Tristram Shandy*). Perhaps the most remarkable example of mock biography is Virginia Woolf's *Orlando* (1928), which—among many other things—ridicules traditional biographical methods. As early as 1780 William Beckford published a satirical collection of mock biographies, *Memoirs of Extraordinary Painters.* See **jest biography, parody biography.**

modernism. A general term marking the period from the late nineteenth century, from Froude, Leslie Stephen, and Gosse, through Lytton Strachey and André Maurois; that is, from the 1880s through the 1930s. The term has been used, with varying inclusive dates, for novels, poetry, drama, and other arts. Major works of modernist biography, following Strachey's *Eminent Victorians* and *Queen Victoria,* shift from traditionalist modes of nineteenth century life-writing to a more artistic brevity and ironic tone characteristic of the new age. New forms and styles, revealing the strong influence of psychological interpretation—Freudian, Jungian, and other—predominate in the period of modernism. Experimental lives, both biographical and autobiographical, reveal changes from heroic to antiheroic, from compilations of facts to mixtures of fact and fiction. Radical breaks from earlier methods can be found in Virginia Woolf's *Orlando,* Lord David Cecil's *Melbourne,* A.J.A. Symons's *The Quest for Corvo,* and Gertrude Stein's *The Autobiography of Alice B. Toklas.* Modern theorists of biography include Lytton Strachey (though he writes little that is more influential than his preface to *Eminent Victorians*), Maurois *(Aspects of Biography),* Woolf (various essays), Gamaliel Bradford (many essays on psychography), and Harold Nicolson *(The Development of English Biography).* For a later account of modernism, see Marshall Berman's *All That is Solid Melts into Air: The Experience of Modernity* (1982). See **postmodernism, theories of life-writing.**

montage. Although this is a technical term in both painting and music, it has also been applied to literary composition, meaning the juxtaposing of various heterogeneous elements; in motion pictures and television, the rapid succession of images to illustrate an association of ideas. In biographical television programs the method of montage has been used with varying degrees of success, but it is a technique that needs further experimentation in visually portraying individual lives. See **cinematic.**

multibiography or **multiple biography.** Lives of two or more persons, published together for some definite purpose. Collections, or groupings, of biographies may vary considerably in numbers, types, arrangement, and so on. Izaak Walton's *Lives of Donne, Wotton, Herbert, Hooker, Sanderson* were originally published separately, but later published together in Walton's own lifetime. A good modern example of thematic grouping of lives is Lytton Strachey's *Eminent Victorians* (1918); also F. L. Lucas's *The Art of Living* (Hume, Horace Walpole, Franklin, Burke) (1959) and *The Search For Good Sense* (Goldsmith, Johnson, Chesterfield, Boswell) (1958) are examples of multibiography. Although the groupings of four lives together is fairly common, one may sometimes find two lives paired (as in Plutarch's parallel lives of Greeks and Romans), as in the modern instances of Lord David Cecil's *Two Quiet Lives* (Dorothy Osborne and Thomas Gray) (1947) and a particularly interesting thematic parallel by two authors, Peter Stansky and William Abrahams, *Journey to the Frontier: Julian Bell and John Cornford: Their Lives and the 1930s* (1966). This is a field of biographical writing that offers considerable opportunity for development; in getting away from mere haphazard collecting into genuinely artistic, thematic interrelationships the biographer can add to the value of one particular life by juxtaposing it to another or several others. There are many examples of multiple biography, but a less common type is that in which several different lives of the same person have been collected (e.g., Helen Darbishire, *The Early Lives of Milton*, 1932; Robert E. Kelley and O M Brack, Jr., *The Early Lives of Samuel Johnson*, 1974; Merton M. Sealts, Jr., *The Early Lives of Melville: Nineteenth-Century Biographical Sketches and Their Authors*, 1974). See **biographical anthology, biographical dictionary, collective lives, dual biography, prosopography, representative.**

multidimensional biography. Portrayal of character in depth and often with opposing characteristics; opposite of **panegyric** or a written composition, usually one dimensional, in praise of a person; in Boswell's words, "to see (Johnson) as he really was." See **stereotype, unidimensional biography.**

multiple selves. Either a figurative term, as used for example, by Virginia Woolf, in her autobiographical essays and diaries, or as a technical term in psychology for cases of people with two or more separate personalities; these subjects have become favorite material for sensational lives.

myth. Old legends of gods and heroes; in life-writing the all-encompassing image for a life, often strongly influenced by Jungian psychology or the works of James G. Frazer, Joseph Campbell, Northrup Frye, Claude Lévi-Straus, and others. See **automythology.**

N

narrative. The recounting of a story; the story-telling element, which varies considerably in individual biographies; the chronological series of events. In a title the word stresses the "story" of the life and may suggest a romantic approach (e.g., *A Narrative of the Life of Mrs. Charlotte Charke*, 1755). In the **psychograph** the chronology is abandoned and as a result there is little or no narrative element. In **fictional biography** the narrative is likely to dominate. See **account, adventures, anecdote.**

narrativity, narratology. The sequence of events in a life, usually presented in chronological order; stress upon telling a tale, a story of a life, applied to both biography and autobiography. "Narratology" was first used in 1969, associated with European Structuralism (Vladimir Propp, *Morphology of the Folktale,* 1928; Gerald Prince, *Narratology,* 1982). See **narrative.**

necrology. List of persons who have died; an ecclesiastical or monastic register containing the deaths of persons connected with or commemorated by a church, monastery, etc.; a death-roll; an obituary notice; the history of the dead. See **epitaph, hagiography, obituary.**

New Biography. In 1927 Virginia Woolf's review of Harold Nicolson's *Some People* was so titled. The term generally refers to the often experimental life-writing done between the two World Wars (1918–1939). The biographers' stress on artistic design, novelistic form, psychological interpretation, and dramatic sequences, by such "new" biographers as Lytton Strachey, André Maurois, Emil Ludwig, and Stefan Zweig, gave the term its popular currency. See Ruth Hoberman, *Modernizing Lives: Experiments in English Biography, 1918–1939* (1987).

noctuary. An account of what passes during the night; a diary of night-time activities.

noneulogistic biography. Infrequently used term for a life that avoids obituary-like praise or encomium; it does not necessarily imply an antagonistic approach by the biographer to the subject.

nonfiction novel. A term used to describe a novel which is closely based on fact, such as Truman Capote's *In Cold Blood.* The term is comparable to, though different from, novelized biography or historical fiction. A nonfiction novel may or may not be biographical, but one may assume that it is based on the actions of actual persons, whether or not fictional names are used. See **biographical novel.**

nostalgia. Originally meaning homesickness, but in the twentieth century its meaning has expanded to include a special kind of memory involving periodic mental states, usually the result of discontinuities in life experience. Not just sentimental memories, nor mere looking back in time, but in the words of Fred Davis *(Yearning for Yesterday: A Sociology of Nostalgia)*, "nostalgia thrives on the subjective apprehension of transition." Times of major change in life provoke nostalgia, even "identity change," or "personal dislocations." Clearly nostalgia is concerned with time and change, and is more evident in autobiography than biography. Diarists and memoirists are prone to recount passages of nostalgia (e.g., Anaïs Nin, Russell Baker), and in plays and films (e.g., Federico Fellini, Neil Simon) nostalgia is pervasive. Davis discusses gender differences, saying that men are more likely to experience nostalgic sequences than are women, because of the distinct discontinuities in their lives (e.g., adolescent break from the father, military service, job status, geographical location). Marcel Proust's nostalgic fiction influences life-writing as well as the novel. The passage of time and the periodicity of history (e.g., the Twenties, the Depression, the Sixties) are also reflected in the individual's personal experience. Related to nostalgia are both adaptation and alienation. See **memory.**

novelized biography. See **biographical novel.**

O

obiter dictum or pl. **obiter dicta.** Incidental opinion or things said in passing (L. "something said by the way"). Comparable to table talk, conversation, and similar informal, unpremeditated comments often recalled in biography. See **conversations, gossip, table talk.**

obituary. A record or announcement of a death or deaths, usually published in a newspaper or current journal or magazine. Some of the best examples are to be found regularly in the *London Times.* Obituaries may vary considerably in length, from hardly more than lists to several hundred words, usually depending on the fame of the deceased. Longer than most obituaries, **memorials** are made by institutional colleagues, nowadays less eulogistic than formerly, but in general friendly in tone (e.g., collection of thirty-one obituaries from the Harvard "Faculty Minutes," *Harvard Scholars in English, 1890–1990*). See **elegy, epitaph, eulogy, hagiography, necrology.**

objective. What is presented to consciousness as opposed to consciousness itself; the purely objective, as opposed to subjective, biography treats its subject so as to exhibit the actual facts, the external events, not colored by the feelings or opinions of the writer. Although objectivity, or detachment, is a desirable quality in a biography, in an extreme form it may interfere with the interpretative function of the work and result in a mere compilation of factual data. All biographical works, even the longest and most detailed, are the result of selection and the process of selection is itself a subjective matter. The parallel between objective and **subjective** is similar to that between **inductive** and **deductive**.

odors. The use of the sense of smell is rare in novels, poetry, and most nonfiction, but in lives of autobiographers the sense of smell is especially related to reminiscences of childhood and youth, perhaps in part because odors are apt to revive in the imagination scenes and places of the past. Among poets Shakespeare and Keats are especially odor-conscious, and biographers of such figures need to be aware of such a characteristic. Edwin Muir's autobiography includes a most effective concern for the sense of smell.

official life. See **life.**

omnium-gatherum. A miscellaneous collection, a medley; accumulation of factual material without any apparent selection; derisive term for some "behemoth" or "super" biographies (Paul Kendall's terms); compilation of source materials for a life. For example, see Gordon Haight's *George Eliot* (1968), William Riley Parker's *Milton* (1968), and Humphrey Carpenter's *Ezra Pound* (1988). See **megabiography.**

opinions. What one thinks or how one thinks about something; belief in something as probable, or as seeming to one's own mind as true, though not certain or established. In the title of a book (Life and Opinions of) it suggests the author's concern with demonstration of evidence in favor of certain opinions; it may also suggest a listing of **sayings, bons mots,** epigrams, and the like. See **-ana.**

oral history. Although the meaning of the term is evident from the two words, it generally now refers to the tape recording of reminiscences about which the narrator can speak with firsthand knowledge. Since the Second World War there have been remarkable advances in oral history and the accumulation of tapes in such major collections as that at Columbia University, where the work of Allan Nevins in the 1940s led to a great hoard of unpublished recollections, a tremendous memory bank of Americana. Elizabeth B. Mason and Louis M. Starr in their book on the *Columbia Oral History Collection* (1973) say that "Biographies make up the largest category of books drawing upon Oral History at Columbia." Other academic institutions are also collecting tapes of oral history; they are, in Bruce Catton's phrase, "creating source materials." It seems likely that oral history will become more and more important in life-writing in the coming decades (see the introduction to T. Harry Williams's *Huey Long,* 1971); in a way it is a compensation for the great decline in letter-writing and for the loss of personal documents in the widespread use of the telephone. An unusual but remarkable illustration of the use of oral material in a biography is Jean Stein's (edited with George Plimpton) *Edie: An American Biography,* 1982; over one hundred characters contribute their comments on Edie Sedgwick and her family; Edie (1943–1971) and her numerous friends (Andy Warhol's entourage) represent a phase of American life, the drug culture, in midcentury. In over four hundred pages, made up entirely of quotations, a central character and her surrounding family and associates are clearly revealed. Many individuals have been presented in oral histories (e.g., *Jack's Book: An Oral History of Jack Kerouac,* by Barry Gifford and Lawrence Lee, 1978). See **conversations, interview.**

otobiography. From otology, the science of the ear; the term is used by Jacques Derrida (*The Ear of the Other: Otobiography, Transference, Translation,* 1985) in his discussion of the ear as a perceiving organ in relation to autobiography and interpretation.

P

pamphlet life. Brief life, often fictional though written in biographical form, published cheaply in paper covers; popular in Elizabethan times, continued in great numbers until they were supplanted by the developing journalism of the late seventeenth and early eighteenth centuries. Pamphlet lives were usually sensational, often concerned with criminals. See **criminal lives.**

panegyric. Formal or elaborate encomium or **eulogy;** in biography, writing devoted to high praise of its subject. See **eulogy, hagiography.**

panoramic. Commanding a view of the whole landscape or continuous passing scene; mental vision in which a series of images passes before the mind's eye. The panoramic method in life-writing is one that gives the background, the overall view of the age in which the subject lives; this method is especially characteristic of historical biography and was practiced to an extreme by Philip Guedalla, where pages of often irrelevant background material were presented. This approach can be used with great effectiveness, as it is in the "Prologue: The World," giving the Whig social and political context for Lord David Cecil's *Melbourne* (1954). Note Leon Edel's description of the "scenic method" (*Literary Biography*, 1957) in dealing with time as handled by biographer and by novelist. See **times**.

parallel lives. Pairs of lives that correspond in some particulars appeared frequently in the seventeenth and eighteenth centuries; all biographies of this type may be said to owe something to Plutarch's *Parallel Lives of Greeks and Romans;* Plutarch wrote forty-six lives, twenty-three pairs, placing one Greek beside one Roman (e.g., Alexander the Great and Julius Caesar; Demosthenes and Cicero) and then, after each pair, writing a brief comparison of the two. See **dual biography**.

parody biography. Imitation of style or subject matter for purposes of ridicule; an unusual form in life-writing, essentially the same as **mock biography**. Virginia Woolf's *Flush* (1933) is at least in part a parody biography, being a view of the Brownings through the eyes of Elizabeth Barrett's cocker spaniel; even more a parody is her *Orlando* (1928), which ridicules conventional biographical methods and techniques; both these works are subtitled "A Biography." Max Beerbohm's *Seven Men* (1919) is a collection of satiric caricatures of literary types more than a parody of biographical methods. William Beckford's *Biographical Memoirs of Extraordinary Painters* (1780) is clearly parodic. See **jest biography, mock biography**.

pathography. Biography or autobiography that emphasizes negative elements in a life: failure, unhappiness, the tragic, and especially illness. See Anne H. Hawkins, *Reconstructing Illness: Studies in Pathography*, 1993: "personal accounts of struggles with chronic, progressive illness and... impending death" (*Times Literary Supplement* review, January 14, 1994). According to Joyce Carol Oates: "hagiography's diminished and often prurient twin." Pathography's "motifs are dysfunction and disaster, illnesses and pratfalls, failed marriages and failed careers, alcoholism and breakdowns and outrageous conduct" (*New York Review of Books*, August 28, 1988, review of David Roberts's life of Jean Stafford).

peepshow biography. Another derogatory term used to characterize lives that sensationalize or diminish a person, in generally short and scandalous accounts, under such titles as *Jackie Oh!* See **potted biographies**.

"perhaps." One of the most used words by biographers; a classic example is the final pages of Lytton Strachey's *Queen Victoria*. Note Bette Lord's comment, "perhaps—that frail pontoon 'perhaps,' on which so many desperate armies have crossed." Along with "perhaps" include "possibly," "may," and "might have." On the other hand, readers should be wary of a biographer's use of such words as "certainly," "undoubtedly," "clearly," "obviously," and "surely." These words may only be the self-reassurance required by the biographer's uncertainty.

48   *Glossary*

But it should be added that guesswork is better accompanied by "perhaps" than with no modifying word at all.

persona. (L. "person"; pl. **personae**). The assumed personality of an author; the speaker in a literary work. Originally used for the list of actors in a drama. The mask is more characteristic of literary forms other than biography and autobiography, but someone like Henry Adams, in using the third person in *The Education of Henry Adams,* was in a way using a persona to avoid subjectivity, or to gain objectivity. Biographers dealing with literary subjects must be especially aware of their subjects' various assumed personalities, the literary personae, in their works, and not confuse the masks with the subject, although they need to understand the subtle relationship that may exist between the person and the masks. See **mask.**

personal essay. Autobiographical essays, or informal short reflections on various aspects of personal experience, were especially popular in the nineteenth century; however, the essay [*essai*] was invented by Montaigne in 1580 and his influence on writing extends down through the centuries, especially as a result of the strongly autobiographical element and the skeptical view of his contemporaries in his *Essais.* See **essay, personal narrative.**

personal heresy. In modern literary criticism, particularly in the opening years of the so-called "New Criticism," one of the major controversies was that between C. S. Lewis and E. M. W. Tillyard on poetry as the expression of the poet's personality. The six articles published in *Essays and Studies* (1934, 1935, 1936) have been collected in *The Personal Heresy: A Controversy* by Oxford University Press (1939; 1965 in paper). Although this discussion has to do with the critical reading of poetry, it is of importance to the biographer of literary figures, particularly in relation to his use of poems, novels, etc. as material for the revelation of character or for the interpretation of his subject. The most obvious danger is the use of fictional material as though it were biographical fact, or the use of poetry written in the first person as though it were straight autobiography. See also *English Institute Essays,* 1946, "The Critical Significance of Biographical Evidence," in which scholars writing on Milton, Swift, Shelley, and Yeats reveal how often biographers and critics misuse biographical material in their interpretations of literary works. The personal heresy is no longer an active controversy, no doubt because reaction to the New Criticism has led to a more modified view of the inevitable relationship between the artist and the creation and because so much recent poetry and fiction is flagrantly autobiographical. The highly responsible use of biographical evidence in modern literary lives is revealed in the work of many contemporary scholars (e.g., Walter Jackson Bate, Richard Ellman, Robert Gittings, Aileen Ward).

personal history. A life history; the whole train of events connected with a particular individual; career; course of existence of a life. Alfred Kazin calls it "my life in history," a characteristically American form. A more general term: personal writings. See **history.**

personalia. Collection of things associated with an individual person; mementoes and personal belongings; in life-writing the term suggests small, personal details. See **-ana, anecdote.**

personality. Distinctive or notable personal character; all the mental, emotional, and social constitutional characteristics of an individual. A "personality cult" may be associated with certain dominating figures either contemporary or from the past. See **hero.**

personal narrative. An account in chronological order of a person's individual life, or part of the life, often dealing with childhood and youth, family relationships, friends, sexual experience, education, and the more intimate than public aspects of a life. See *First Person Singular,* a collection edited by Charles Muscatine and Marlene Griffith, 1973. See **personal history.**

photoanalysis. The interpretation of photographs, family snapshots and the like, from a psychoanalytical point of view. As Oliver Wendell Holmes once said, photographs are like mirrors with memories. See Robert U. Akeret, *Photoanalysis* (1973), an analysis of 230 photos showing the unconscious meanings of gestures, posture, expressions. Like handwriting analysis and "body language," photoanalysis is a popular method—part science, part game—of trying to understand other human beings. See **iconography.**

photobiography. A life presented in photographs or the life of a photographer, including the interrelationships among the photographer, the photos, and the subjects of the photos (e.g., Margaret Bourke-White, Edward Steichen); a life of a subject with extensive use of portraits and personal photographs. Pictorial lives have grown along with photobiography. Thames and Hudson publishers (London) have put out a series of fully illustrated biographies which include portraits, paintings, photos, and snapshots of the subject and related figures, homes, landscapes, and samples of handwriting (e.g., Harry T. Moore's *D. H. Lawrence* and *Henry James and His World*). An increasingly popular type of biography, the illustrated life has been stimulated by portraits taken by fine photographers (Cecil Beaton, Karsh, Richard Avedon), and by the work of scholars dealing with the relationship between author images and life story (e.g., David Piper's *The English Face;* Richard Wendorf's *The Elements of Life*). See **iconography, portrait, profile.**

phrenology. A theory that one's mental powers are revealed by the shape of the skull; that the brain, consisting of a number of organs, corresponding to faculties of the mind, indicates the powers of the individual, the mental characteristics and capacities; that these powers can be determined by observing the prominence of areas on the surface of the skull; as a branch of biological science called "craniology." The pseudoscience of phrenology was popular in the nineteenth century, derived in part from the influence of John Lavater, who was actually a physiognomist rather than a phrenologist. Reed Whittemore points out that the nineteenth century American biographer James Parton used "the fashionable phrenological judgments of the period" describing Horace Greeley's brain as being "of the best form, long, narrow and high," indicating "small animality and selfishness, extreme benevolence, natural nobleness and loftiness of aim." Parton may have been making fun, but he does refer to phrenology often. In modern times Gordon S. Haight's *George Eliot* deals with her interest in phrenology. See **face reading, physiognomy.**

physiognomy. The face or countenance considered as an index of character; the features of the face (sometimes even the form and structure of the body generally) as a means of determining personality. John (or Johan) Gaspar Lavater (1741–1801) had a widespread influence throughout Europe through his publications beginning in the 1770s; "My endeavours," he says, "have been directed to define the peculiarities of each part of the countenance." Lavater gave rules, many illustrations, and examples, including even a chart that showed the "human" countenance from a frog to Apollo; he lists "remarkable countenances" and has an essay on portrait painting. Lavater influenced the later pseudoscience of **phrenology.** He was Swiss and a friend of the artist Henry Fuseli; he is certainly among the most curious figures in the history of western Europe. Biographers in modern times are not concerned with phrenology, but through the use of iconographical aids in life-writing, the analysis of how a character looked becomes more evident. The metaphorical use of a mask is of course related to the actual face. See **face reading, iconography, phrenology.**

political biography. Many historical biographies are political as well, but as a category the type is mainly concerned with governmental action, party (often partisan), and the life and actions of a politician. Military lives often include political material. The usual subjects are leaders (generals, presidents, dictators), though less powerful figures (ambassadors, cabinet members, legislative leaders) are often subjects—as well as autobiographers—of political lives. Justification for past political action is often the motive for political memoirs. Postwar periods often lead to biographies that revise judgments on political careers (e.g., John Charmley, *Churchill: The End of Glory, A Political Biography,* 1993). See **campaign lives, revisionist biography.**

portrait. A likeness; in biography, a word picture, a verbal representation, a vivid description. If the word "portrait" is applied to the whole biographical work, it suggests less concern with narrative and more with personality (e.g., Lytton Strachey's *Portraits in Miniature,* 1931). The portrait as painting is often used as illustrative supplement to a biography, as frontispiece, or throughout a life with other illustrative material, especially in modern biographies. A marked departure in the sophisticated examination of the relation between images and lives is Richard Wendorf's *The Elements of Life: Biography and Portrait-Painting in Stuart and Georgian England* (1990). See **iconography, miniature, profile.**

postmodernism. The period after World War II generally marks the beginning of postmodernism, when continued experimentation in life-writing and further nontraditional methods spread more widely than before. Brevity was no longer regarded as essential. Evident as early as the criticism of Leslie Fiedler and Ihab Hassan, postmodernism can be seen as both an extension of modernism and as antimodernism. Applied at first mainly to art and architecture, it is also applied to literature, although more frequently to the novel than to biography. Literature of the absurd, antihistorical, and that which undermines the conventional or traditional in life-writing can be included within the wide range of the postmodern. The antihero and the alienated, perhaps most frequently revealed in autobiography, are characteristic types. Norman Mailer, Frank Conroy, and Lillian Hellman express these aspects in their autobiographical works. As early as 1941 Vladimir Nabokov's novel *The Real Life of Sebastian Knight* deals with aspects of life-writing that concern later postmodern theorists (e.g., "Remember that what you are told is really threefold: shaped by the teller, reshaped by the listener, concealed from both by the dead man of the tale;" the opening paragraph of Chapter 6). Another experimental type is Steven Millhauser's *Edwin Mullhouse:The Life and Death of an American Writer, 1943–1954, by Jeffrey Cartwright* (1972), actually a novel which, like Virginia Woolf's *Orlando,* claims "that the very notion of biography (is) hopelessly fictional;" that it is "unlike real life." The concept of truth itself is abandoned by poststructuralism (see Frederic Jameson, *Postmodernism,* 1991), and interpretation, which was so significant to Freudians, is repudiated. Norman Mailer's *Marilyn* (1973) illustrates these rejections. Although postmodernism influences culture as a whole, life-writing as a genre reflects its influence less obviously than art, architecture, and the novel. See **deconstruction, modernism, theories of life-writing.**

potted biographies. A derisive term used by reviewers in the *Times Literary Supplement* (e.g., January 26, 1973, and June 20, 1975) for uninspired biographies which are routinely prepared—though well packed with factual information. As early as November 1929 Kipling used the term in a letter. Other derisive terms used by reviewers in weekly journals such as *Time*, the *Times Literary Supplement*, and the *New York Review of Books* include "plaster cast" biography and "what Katy did next" autobiography.

prison autobiography. Personal accounts written while in prison or about one's time of imprisonment. Such works vary from classical lives to modern criminal stories. Tales written in prison, such as Malory's *Morte D'arthur* or Bunyan's *Pilgrim's Progress* are not within this category, but Bunyan's *Grace Abounding* and Hitler's *Mein Kampf* represent two extremes of the type. In more recent times *Soledad Brother: The Prison Letters of George Jackson* (1970) and Jacobo Timmerman's *Prisoner Without a Name, Cell Without a Number* (1981) are representative; female experiences are seen in Jean S. Harris, *Always Call Us Ladies: Stories From Prison* (1988).

private life. Intimate, personal life of a subject in biography; opposite to the public life. Even Plutarch (see his "Alexander the Great") recognized the significance of the private, or domestic, aspect of a life, particularly as opposed to history, but only in the seventeenth century did extensive presentation of private life come into biography. The intimate family memoirs of seventeenth-century writers (e.g., Lady Anne Fanshawe, Lucy Hutchinson) who wrote not for publication, but for their children and descendants, led the way toward more intimate lives in the eighteenth century. Roger North, in writing of his three brothers (1715), makes a point of revealing private matters. See also Dryden's *Life of Plutarch*, prefaced to the new translation of Plutarch in 1683. In modern times, especially since Strachey, the private element has been stressed in life-writing, often in the period of the 1920s and 1930s suggesting scandalous or sensational material. See **scandal.**

professional biographer. One whose essential career is writing lives. Although Izaak Walton or Daniel Defoe might be called "first," clearly the nineteenth century produced the first in John Forster (1812–1876), whose many biographies, especially that of Dickens, made him a successful professional. Contemporaries Samuel Smiles (1812–1904) and Leslie Stephen (1832–1904) were both writers of numerous lives, and notably successful in making a living thereby. In America James Parton (1822–1891) as a career wrote many lives of American historical figures. In the twentieth century professional biographers have become ever more numerous: among others Lytton Strachey, Gamaliel Bradford, Emil Ludwig, Stefan Zweig, Hesketh Pearson, and in the latter part of the century, Edward Wagenknecht, Virginia Cowles, Antonia Fraser, Charles Higham, and Justin Kaplan. See Ira B. Nadel's chapter "Biography as a Profession" in his *Biography: Fiction, Fact, and Form* (1984).

profile. The outline, or contour, of anything; the outline of the human face seen from the side; in biography, a brief sketch professing to give only the outlines of a character and a life. In modern times the name has often been used for collections of short biographies (e.g., John F. Kennedy's *Profiles in Courage,* 1956). The *New Yorker* magazine has for many years regularly published rather long profiles. See **miniature, portrait, silhouette.**

propaganda. Lives written for propagandistic purposes are numerous, though not always obvious. Any systematic or concerted attempt to establish a particular image of a person is likely to come under the heading of propaganda; **campaign lives** (see Hawthorne on Franklin Pierce), political lives, biographies of leaders of religions (see Mormon establishment lives of Joseph Smith or Brigham Young, or Christian Science church-sponsored lives of Mary Baker Eddy)—all are, in varying degrees, propagandistic. Sometimes in the field of literary life-writing one detects propagandistic motives, as in *Providence and Mr. Hardy,* by Lois Deacon and Terry Coleman (1966) or in controversial biographical studies of Sylvia Plath.

prosopography. Collective biography, but suggesting a group of lives with common background characteristics; a collective study of the lives of a particular group. Though this term has been used in modern times and seems to be appearing more frequently it is not in dictionaries generally and it is listed in the *Oxford English Dictionary* as obsolete, with a definition as follows: "a description of the person or personal appearance," an inadequate definition of the word as it is now sometimes used. Lawrence Stone, in an article called "Prosopography" (*Daedalus,* Winter 1971, pp. 46–49), defines the word as "the investigation of the common background characteristics of a group of actors in history by means of a collective study of their lives;" later on Stone says that the "three most brilliant examples of prosopographical research on political elites" are Syme's *Roman Revolution,* Namier's *Structure of Politics,* and Sir John Neale's great trilogy on the Elizabethan House of Commons. See also A. H. M. Jones, J. R. Martindale, and J. Morris, *The Prosopography of the Later Roman Empire,* Vol. I *A.D. 260–395* (1971). See **collective lives, group biography, multibiography.**

prosopolatria. Face worship; comparable to *idolatria* or the worship of men; see Sacvan Bercovitch, *The Puritan Origins of the American Self* (1975), in which Cotton Mather's *Life of John Winthrop* is cited. See **eulogy.**

prototypes. Original, model, ideal subjects in life-writing; these may derive from historical, fictional, religious, or mythical figures used to describe character; e.g., Faustian, Byronic, Promethean. See **character, typology.**

pseudoautobiographic. A term more often used about novels, such as picaresque narratives, than about biography; first-person novels, such as those by Defoe, are often so designated.

pseudonymity. The practice of using a pseudonym, a pen name, or *nom de plume*, more often used by novelists than by biographers or autobiographers.

psychoanalysis. A system of medical practice, introduced by Freud, that interprets and treats disorders through the investigation of the unconscious side of mental life. Psychoanalysis has greatly influenced biography in the twentieth century, since the science adds a new means of achieving comprehension of the subjects of lives. Many sensational and confessional lives in the 1920s and later utilize this method with varying degrees of responsibility and with widely different interpretations. Always a controversial method (witness some of the responses to Leon Edel's *Henry James,* 1953–1972), it has nevertheless become more responsible, more restrained, in recent years. The rash of debunking biographies in the 1920s used presumed Freudian approaches for sensational purposes only. It is best to begin the study of the application of psychoanalysis to life-writing by reading Freud's own *Leonardo da Vinci: A Study in Psychosexuality* (1910), where his claims are far more modest than those of his so-called followers. See discussions in Ernest Jones, *Freud* (1953–1957), and in Peter Gay, *Freud* (1988). See **case studies.**

psychobiography. A psychological biography; to be clearly distinguished from **psychography,** a term in literary art, whereas **psychobiography** designates a scientific approach to the subject through psychological methods; comparable to **psychohistory.** An analysis of the psychological makeup of an individual, revealing motivation and ultimately essential character, is the basis for psychobiography. The influence of Freud's psychoanalysis is reflected in one of the early psychobiographers, Erik Erikson, who in his *Young Man Luther* (1958) applies this method, establishing the influential term "identity crisis" and related concepts in his biographical work. See Erikson's *Life History and the Historical Moment* (1975). Lytton Strachey's *Elizabeth and Essex* reveals the influence of Freud's psychoanalytic methods. Adverse criticism of psychobiography was characteristic of the middle decades of this century, but by the 1970s the idea of interpreting a life rather than merely reporting it was widely recognized and clearly represented in the work of such psychobiographers as Bruce Mazlish and Leon Edel, in frequent articles in *Biography,* and in books on theories of life-writing (e.g., Chapter 6 in Ira Bruce Nadel's *Biography: Fiction, Fact, and Form,* 1984). See **pathography, psychoanalysis.**

psychography. The history, description, or delineation of the mind, or soul, or the presentation of character. The term was first used by St. Beuve, but it was introduced, defined, and much written about by

Gamaliel Bradford (1863–1932) in the early decades of the twentieth century. Bradford seeks to extract the essentials from a person's life, disregarding chronological order of events and achieving unity by weaving his discussion around dominant themes. The psychograph became a highly formalized method of writing short lives (about 30,000 words) often grouped in one volume (*Damaged Souls,* 1923; *Wives,* 1925; *Daughters of Eve,* 1930). The chronology of the life was given as a list at the beginning of the sketch, with perhaps an early paragraph devoted to the entire sequence of events in a life, from birth to death; then, as a kind of series of concentric circles such themes as religion, money, or ambition, were selected as the psychographer discussed the subject, with very little by way of anecdote or concrete detail. The method of psychography has sometimes been used, even by Bradford himself (Robert E. Lee), for full-length lives, especially by Bradford's close follower and perhaps the only active psychographer in recent years, Edward Wagenknecht (*Henry Wadsworth Longfellow: Portrait of an American Humanist,* 1966; *John Greenleaf Whittier: A Portrait in Paradox,* 1967). The psychograph should not be confused with modern psychological methods in life-writing; the "psycho" here derives from the Greek word for "soul," psyche. The word "soul" appears frequently in Bradford titles and the word "portrait" is also often used in titles of psychographs.

psychohistory. Originally "applying psychology to history"; a history of the psyche; now a separate area of study (see Lloyd deMause, ed., *A Bibliography of Psychohistory,* 1975), a "new science of patterns of historical motivations," based on psychological studies of childhood and closely associated with Erik Erikson's theories. See **psychobiography.**

pure (and **impure**) **biography.** A distinction made by Harold Nicolson (*The Development of English Biography,* 1928) to clarify the difference between "the truthful and deliberate record of an individual's life written as a work of intelligence" from those lives that confuse by "elements extraneous to the art itself," such as **hagiography,** illustrating a theory, or being unduly subjective. Nicolson was defining these terms at a time when the "New Biography" was introducing many confusing elements into life-writing.

Q

quest. A search or pursuit in order to find out something; occasionally this word is used in the title of a biographical work, suggesting an emphasis upon the biographer's problem in finding out about the subject. A. J. A. Symons' *The Quest for Corvo* (1934) is perhaps the best example of this use of the term. Symons' method is to portray Frederic William Rolfe (Baron Corvo) not in chronological order of his life, but as Symons himself discovers, and pursues, the character of the man. This novel method is carried through only the first third of the book; from Chapter 8 on, more conventional methods are used, but it is an interesting experimental approach to life-writing. Another kind of quest is that represented in *The Quest for Arthur Conan Doyle: Thirteen Biographers in Search of a Life*, edited by Jon L. Lellenberg. Other variants of the type are Frederick Pottle's *Pride and Negligence: The History of the Boswell Papers* (1982) and David Buchanan's *The Treasures of Auchinleck* (1974).

R

recollections. Accounts of events or persons recalled to the mind in later years. Recollections have always formed an important part of autobiography and of that biography which is dependent upon personal knowledge of the subject (e.g., Boswell on Johnson, Lockhart on Scott, Froude on Carlyle). The word is often used in autobiographical titles, especially in the nineteenth century (e.g., Edward Trelawny, *Recollections of the Last Days of Shelley and Byron*, 1858; John Morley, *Recollections*, 1917). See **autobiography, reminiscences.**

reminiscences. Collective memories of personal experiences put into literary form; recollections; remembrances. Another favorite nineteenth-century title (e.g., Thomas Carlyle, *Reminiscences*, 1866; Henry Crabb Robinson, *Reminiscences and Correspondence*, 1869). See **autobiography, recollections.**

repartee. A ready, witty reply; witticism. See **bon mot.**

repentance. Sorrow for wrongdoing with a desire to cease sinning, often the motivation for writing autobiography, confessional autobiography. Repentance may be pretended, especially as prefatory to a sensational or scandalous autobiographical account. The term is usually found in early life-writing, but the spirit is characteristic of all confessional writing (e.g., *The Book of Margery Kempe*, 1436, pub. 1936; *The Repentance of Robert Greene*, 1572). See **confessions.**

representative. Standing for, portraying, symbolizing, conveying an adequate idea of, in a prominent or comprehensive manner; typical embodiment of. Lives have often been collected on the basis of their representativeness of their class or period or profession. Representative men have been favorite subjects for life-writing especially in the nineteenth and early twentieth centuries (e.g., Ralph Waldo Emerson, *Representative Men*, 1850, similar to and perhaps inspired by Thomas Carlyle, *Heroes and Hero-Worship*, 1841; Lytton Strachey, *Eminent Victorians*, 1918; Anne K. Tuell, *John Sterling; A Representative Victorian*, 1941).

reputation. The general estimation of a person by others. Reputations rise and fall; such fluctuations influence the production of lives by biographers, especially professional writers, usually influenced by the sales figures of publishers. Major subjects tend to be widely recognized at the end of their careers and biographies appear shortly after their deaths. Reputations, or popularity, then tends to decline for a number of years, sometimes quite rapidly, sometimes permanently. Anniversaries, new discoveries, or just chance may revive a reputation and bring forth new biographies. An example of long delay is that of John Donne, whose life was written by Izaak Walton in 1640, shortly after Donne's death; for about 150 years Donne remained relatively unknown and then his reputation rose rapidly for decades. There are those who recommend that the best time for a biographer to undertake the task is about ten years after a subject's death. Reputation, of course, does not necessarily mean celebrity; some reputations are related to individual peculiarity, as biographers are presumably aware. See Leo Braudy, *The Frenzy of Renown: Fame and Its History* (1986).

revisionist biography. A modern term for a major change in the biography of a major figure; a departure from the traditional, generally accepted view of a subject, often the result of new material or interpretation of a life. See **counterbiography, doubts.**

roman à clef. (Fr., lit., novel with a key.) Novel in which actual persons, places, and events are disguised as fiction. Although such works are often written as a means of avoiding libel suits or as a way of dealing with scandalous material in a partially covered up manner, they may often be biographical or historical and are sometimes, long afterwards, republished with the key to names and places indicated at the beginning (e.g., Aldous Huxley, *Point Counter Point*, 1928). See **biographical novel.**

romantic biography. Comparable to romance in fiction or the novel. Extravagant stories of exciting adventures, with scenes remote from ordinary life; romantic life-writing is a persistent form, though it is more popular in some periods than in others, perhaps especially in the late eighteenth and early nineteenth centuries and in the modern period after the early biographies by André Maurois (*Ariel*, 1923; *Disraeli*, 1927; *Byron*, 1930). In general, romantic biography is undependable, fictionalized, and entertaining. The American explorer and writer Richard Halliburton (1900–1939) popularized an autobiographical version of romantic life-writing in the twenties and thirties with such books as *The Royal Road to Romance* (1925), *The Glorious Adventure* (1927), and *New Worlds to Conquer* (1929). See **adventures, autonovel, biographical novel.**

roots. Ancestors; antecedents; derived from the metaphorical use of the roots of a tree; source. The term has become especially popular for family, or genealogical, research since Alex Haley's book and television program, *Roots* (1976). See **genealogy.**

royal lives. Lives of kings and queens. Royal lives were among the earliest works, although often they were largely chronicles of the reign rather than individualized lives. In England one of the first royal lives to reveal an individual personality was an anonymous life of Henry V (1513). Even today, when royalty has long since passed its heyday, lives of former kings and queens, princes and princesses, and current monarchs are among the most popular subjects. Royal marriages and divorces bring forth myriads of romantic and scandalous biographies. Witness the many books on the Windsors, from Edward's abdication to Diana's unhappy life.

S

sacred lives. Early lives of saints, hagiography. See Frank E. Reynolds and Donald E. Capps, eds., *The Biographical Process: Studies in the History and Psychology of Religion* (1976). See **hagiography.**

saints' lives. See **hagiography.**

sayings. Things said by a (more or less distinguished) person; apothegms; dicta. See **conversations, gossip, obiter dictum, table talk.**

scandal. Defamation or discrediting of character by means of vituperative or shocking revelations; disgrace, ill-repute, obloquy. The creation of scandal is not generally considered a legitimate purpose for biography, but it has been an element of life-writing for centuries. Perhaps the earliest famous scandalous lives are Suetonius's *Lives of the Twelve Caesars* (ca. A.D. 121), but the earliest vituperative biography in England was Thomas More's *Richard III*, written in his youth at the request of Archbishop Morton as part of the Tudor propaganda. All scandal is not necessarily based on false evidence. Most lives have skeletons in the closet somewhere, and although the eighteenth century life-writers took their scandals in stride, the nineteenth century biographers, often in prudish reticence, held back material that in another age would hardly raise an eyebrow. The reticence led to a different sort of scandal when modern scholars uncovered the facts, laid bare the details, and revealed the cover-ups of earlier biographers. Witness such cases as Wordsworth and Annette Vallon, Byron's incestuous relation with his half-sister, Dickens' affair with Ellen Ternan, and Carlyle's impotence. Scandal has, of course, a stronger impact immediately after the death of the subject, when first biographies are written, but as time goes on the shock becomes less dramatic, the scandal less scandalous, and eventually the scandal is not so much the facts left untold, but the fact of the concealment. In more recent times biographical scandal has had its active share in the public press, as for example the Clifford Irving hoax biography of Howard Hughes, the noisy controversy over William Manchester's book on the assassination of President Kennedy, or the revelation of Franklin D. Roosevelt's extramarital affair. In the twentieth century, libel laws have interfered with frank reporting of contemporary or nearly contemporary lives. Scandal is a complex term, perhaps more often implying, to the perceptive reader, lies, or untruth, rather than fact, but always sensationally popular with less thoughtful, casual readers. Sometimes a scandalous biography avoids legal suit by the biographer being aware that a legal attack would make the situation worse for the subject; witness Joe McGinniss, *The Last Brother: The Rise and Fall of Ted Kennedy* (1993). The use of the word "scandal" in a title may improve the book's sales (e.g., Alan Chedzoy's *A Scandalous Woman: The Story of Caroline Norton*, 1992).

scholarly biography. Thorough, systematic, documented study and presentation of lives with selection and design. The scholarly biography uses original, or primary, sources and is careful to cite evidence. The tradition of scholarly life-writing begins with the antiquarians of the sixteenth century and develops up through the eighteenth and nineteenth centuries, part of the scientific advance represented so clearly in nineteenth century German scholarship, reaching an admirable climax in the present age. Although one could cite such scholarly life-writers as Samuel Johnson, Edmund Malone, and James A. Froude, the more obvious representatives would come from the twentieth century: Mark Schorer on Sinclair Lewis, Leslie Marchand on Byron, Leon Edel on Henry James, Carlos Baker on Ernest Hemingway, Aileen Ward on Keats, the various lives by Richard Ellmann, or Walter Jackson Bates on Johnson. See **documentation, life.**

scientific biography. A method of writing suggesting a detached, objective, perhaps even uncritical approach; the inductive method generally, although it may in effect be confirmation of hypotheses.

Scientific, for some readers, implies scholarly. The term is also used of lives of or by scientists. See **inductive.**

scrappiana. Sir Sydney Robert's term for much of what appears in J. L. Clifford and Donald Greene's bibliography of Johnsonian studies. Odds and ends of miscellaneous items; "scraps" relating, however remotely, to the subject of a biography.

secret life. A term sometimes used to suggest scandal, sensationalism, in order to sell the book; Hollywood lives, written by gossip columnists, or ghostwritten autobiographies often use this label. However, probably the most famous use of the title, *My Secret Life,* is that of the anonymous nineteenth century English gentleman who kept a diary of his sexual escapades over many years. The book was published in 1888 and became a subject of controversial censorship for many years. It has been called the longest erotic autobiography ever written.

sectarian autobiography. Certain religious sects developed conventions for presenting individual religious experiences (see Paul Delany, *British Autobiography in the Seventeenth Century*). Many such self-stories were written in seventeenth and eighteenth century England and America. See **confessions, spiritual autobiography, testimony.**

selection. The inevitable process in any life-writing, long or short; the art of leaving out (Edel); the "new biography," from Strachey on, was particularly concerned with the art of selection. See **New Biography.**

self-analysis. Introspection; examination and evaluation of one's mental state and processes; analytical autobiography. See **autobiography.**

self-biography. Rarely used term for which an unnamed reviewer in the British *Monthly Review* (1796) offered the newly created word **autobiography** as a replacement. The variety of terms used for autobiographical writings indicates that autobiography cannot easily be classified as a single genre; rather it is a cluster of genres, varying greatly in form and in style. See **autobiography.**

self-discovery. A descriptive term for some autobiographical writings, comparable to "self-scrutiny" or even the more general term "self-writing." The implication of "discovery" is that the autobiography reveals analysis, more concern with mental aspects than with external events or anecdotes. See **self-analysis.**

self-study. Another term for **self-analysis.**

self-writing. An infrequently used word for **autobiography,** although the term can include any writing that is autobiographical in nature. Perhaps the most active field of scholarly research in life-writing today is on self-writing, particularly as it relates to fiction.

sequentiality. Narrative material in logical order, cause and effect, or sequence of time **(chronology).** Most life-writing has been in the order of time, but debate continues over which approach is to be preferred, topical or chronological. See **psychograph.**

serial autobiography. Robert A. Fothergill's term (*Private Chronicles: A Study of English Diaries,* 1974) for diary writing that covers fairly continuously a number of years with "autobiographical consciousness" on the part of the diarist and the presentation of an organic story, perhaps combining **autobiography** and **diary** (e.g., Benjamin Robert Haydon's *Autobiography and Journals*). The term also applies to series of autobiographical works, usually published over a number of years, in either chronological or topical order, as the several volumes by Osbert Sitwell, Ved Mehta, Leonard Woolf, Maya Angelou, and May Sarton illustrate. See **diary.**

series. Separate publication of lives grouped in some way, as in the English Men of Letters series. See **collective lives, multibiography.**

sermon. Although a sermon is a discourse delivered from the pulpit, based on a text of scripture and giving instruction or exhortation, the early saints' lives were often designed for use as sermons, or within the sermon, particularly as part of the service of the saint's fete day, or day of commemoration. The didactic element in life-writing has always been used by the preacher as part of his sermon, and the Gospels are themselves biographical; parables are often biographical in nature, though they may be limited to an incident or anecdote. The term *sermonizing* in relation to biography is a contemptuous or derisive one, suggesting that the life is a long or tedious harangue, with little real value as a life. See **exemplum, fall, hagiography.**

silhouette. Like the word **profile,** signifying a slight sketch of a person, the outline only. See **profile, portrait, sketch, vignette.**

simplex autobiography. James Olney separates autobiographers into two large groups: simplex and duplex. In the single metaphor type each has "his own daimon, his personal genius and guardian spirit" (Fox, Darwin, Mill). See James Olney's *Metaphors of Self,* 1972. See **duplex autobiography.**

sketch. A brief account, description, or narrative giving the main or important facts or incidents, but not going into details. In life-writing the term always means brevity; sometimes it implies light or rapid handling of a life, bordering upon the superficial and the unfinished (e.g., George Bernard Shaw, *Sixteen Self-Sketches,* 1949). See **cameo, portrait, profile, silhouette, vignette.**

slave narrative. As early as 1830 accounts of escaped slaves, generally rather brief, were published, often under the auspices of abolition societies. William L. Andrews calls Briton Hammon's fourteen-page account in 1760 the first. This form became popular as a "captivity" narrative (cf. also Indian stories, 1680–1760, often with a Christian vs. Savage theme). Antebellum stories were followed after the Civil War by longer autobiographies, especially by former slaves who succeeded in the world, such as Booker T. Washington's *Up From Slavery*

(1901). One of the most influential was Frederick Douglass's 1881 autobiography, frequently reprinted. Louis Kaplan's bibliography of American autobiographies lists over seventy slave autobiographies. See **African American life-writing, black life-writing.**

sociobiography. A biography that stresses the social background or milieu of the subject and may stress the sociological elements of the subject's life, revealing the interaction of the individual life with the environment. Such a life may be more concerned with didactic effect than it is with the recreation of a life. See **Marxist biography, prosopography.**

speeches. See **conversations.**

spiritual autobiography. Account of one's religious experience, of one's relationship to God. Characteristic of early American autobiographical works, whether diaries, journals, or autobiographies, are the revelations of spiritual condition, often concerned with the question of grace (e.g., Michael Wigglesworth's *Diary*, John Woolman's *Journal*, Jonathan Edwards' *Personal Narrative*). Quaker and Puritan spiritual records were especially prevalent in the seventeenth century, but spiritual autobiography can be found from St. Augustine to Cardinal Newman and Thomas Merton. (See G. A. Starr, *Defoe and Spiritual Autobiography*, 1965). See **autobiography, sectarian autobiography.**

standard life. See **life.**

stereotype. Conforming to a fixed pattern; a person whose character is fixed as a general type, perhaps by the first biographical study of the subject. The term is becoming ever more pejorative in the current attempts to avoid labeling national or sexual stereotypes. Biographical stereotypes are best seen in "representative men" (a popular nineteenth century approach, as in Carlyle or Emerson) and possibly at the worst in fixed conceptions of figures as "villains" or "heroes." See **hero, vituperative biography.**

subject. The person about whom a biography is written.

subjective. See **objective.**

T

table talk. Talk at table, or familiar conversation at meals, ordinary gossip; the social conversation of famous men or interesting groups especially in literary form, often collected and published separately from other biographical material. It may form an important part of complete biographies, as notably in Boswell's *Johnson*. Characteristically a nineteenth century term (e.g., William Hazlitt, *Table Talk, or Original Essays on Men and Manners,* 1821–1822), but note also Martin Luther's *Table Talk* (1568). See **conversations, gossip.**

testamentary acts. From Michael Millgate's book of that title (1992). Although wills are the most obvious—and often among the most important—remains of a biographical subject, letters, diaries, manuscripts, and various editions of works are also significant, especially for literary executors. Millgate deals with four major writers (Browning, Tennyson, James, and Hardy), all of whom lived to an old age and were concerned with posthumous publications of their works, as well as with their biographers. This is a large and surprisingly relatively unexplored area of importance to biographers. In Millgate's terms, "executorial actions of every kind, though referred to the dead and to the past, signify only within the present and the future." See **eulogy, obituary, wills.**

testimony. Open attestation or acknowledgment; confession or profession; bearing witness, testifying. This term in life-writing suggests giving personal evidence. Religious autobiography, particularly that of the Quakers in the seventeenth century and thereafter, was testimonial, or giving evidence of the personal experience of the deity, of God's grace. Perhaps the best example of testimonial autobiography is John Bunyan's *Grace Abounding to the Chief of Sinners* (1666). The nearest thing to a school of autobiographies (on the face of it an anomaly) is the testimonial lives by the followers of George Fox, whose journal (1694) served as a model for the Society of Friends.

textual biography. The history of a creative writer's works dealing in chronological order with the stages of development, from manuscripts and typescripts through serialization, editions, collections; and involving editors, publishers, printers, and others. Authors' revisions and relationships to their editors are important aspects of their literary careers and may be of great significance to their biographers (e.g., Henry James and his New York edition). Though editing principles (Walter Greg, Fredson Bowers, G. T. Tanselle) may involve highly technical material, obviously avoided by the popular biographer, the definitive biography of a novelist, poet, or dramatist may well require such concern. See Simon Gatrell, *Hardy the Creator: A Textual Biography* (1988). See **bio-bibliography, testamentary acts.**

theories of life-writing. From Lytton Strachey to Leon Edel the twentieth century has been increasingly concerned with theories of biography and autobiography. If the eighteenth century had the Johnson/Boswell central figures in biographical theory and the nineteenth century had the Carlyle/Leslie Stephen figures as major theorists of life-writing, the twentieth century has no such clear concentration on any particular individuals as the prominent theorists. However, there have been many astute critics of life-writing, especially in recent years in autobiography. To name only a few of the books which present these theorists in clear and informative fashion, they include James Clifford, *Biography as an Art* (1962), David Novarr, *The Lines of Life: Theories of Biography, 1880–1970* (1986), Richard Ellmann, *Golden Codgers: Biographical Speculations* (1973), and Ira B. Nadel, *Biography: Fiction, Fact, and Form* (1984). See **autobiography, biography.**

times. The historical period in which a person lives; the *life and times* is a characteristic form of nineteenth century biography, recording not only the individual's career, but also the historical events that accompanied it, thus combining biography and history (e.g., John Thomas Smith, *Nollekens and His Times,* 1828; John Forster, *The Life and Times of Oliver Goldsmith,* 1854; Winston Churchill, *Marlborough, His Life and Times,* 1933–1938). See **life, panoramic.**

tour. Going or traveling from place to place; an excursion, or journey, visiting places in a circuit or sequence. A popular form in the eighteenth century was the journal of a tour, at a time when the Grand Tour, meaning a journey through France, Germany, Switzerland, and Italy, was fashionable as a kind of finishing course in the education of young English gentlemen of rank. These were generally long journeys, covering from one to three years, perhaps involving the keeping of a diary or journal (e.g., Boswell's *Journal of a Tour to Corsica,* 1768). See **journal, travels, voyages, Wanderjahr.**

transference. The relation of the biographer to the subject; originally from psychoanalysis, on the emotional attitude of the patient toward the analyst. See Leon Edel, *Writing Lives: Principia Biographica,* where he deals at length with the emotional involvement of the biographer with the subject, usually one of "affection and love" but possibly even animosity. Most unlikely is complete indifference. See **collaboration.**

travels. An account of occurrences and observations of a journey, usually into foreign parts; as facility in travel increased, accounts of journeys and travels became more extensive and more distant than tours. In the nineteenth century travels is more frequent in titles than tours (e.g., Charles M. Doughty, *Travels in Arabia Deserta,* 1888). See **tour, voyages.**

truncated biography. An unusual term for a partial life (e.g., *The Early Career of Alexander Pope,* by George Sherburn, who did not live to complete a second volume); it has a slightly pejorative sense in that it suggests a fragment of a statue, or that the life lacks a proper ending. See **profile, sketch.**

typology. The study of types, the classification of types. "Character typology" is a general term used for the classification of psychological types; any system of classification, from zodiacal and phrenological to Eriksonian categories of childhood, which deals with human beings, with personality, on the basis of some pattern or overall grouping. The word originally concerns symbolism and no doubt one would do better to speak of "character types" rather than of "typology." See **character.**

U

unauthorized biography. Letters columns in literary periodicals make evident the constant problem of lives written against the wishes of families and friends, not to mention the subjects themselves. Many famous persons did everything possible to prevent biographies being written (e.g., Henry James, T. S. Eliot, W. H. Auden). Survivors, especially widows, have frequently not only refused to give any help but have attempted by legal means to prevent lives from being written. In recent times the Orwell and Plath controversies have been widely publicized, as well as the T. S. Eliot affair (e.g., Peter Ackroyd's biography). Being authorized or unauthorized generally has no essential relationship to the value of the life written. See **authorized biography, widow biography.**

unidimensional biography. A surface approach to life-writing, stereotyping, "constructing a life so it fits into and illustrates some prior conception or didactic point the biographer wishes to press," as Richard A. Hutch points out in "Strategic Irony and Lytton Strachey's Contribution to Biography," *Biography* 11, no. 1 (Winter 1988). See **multidimensional biography.**

V

"valet biography." Another denigrating term to describe iconoclastic life-writing; "no man is a hero to his valet" (a saying as old as Antigonus, but note Montaigne's "Few men have been admired by their own domestics"). This term suggests a life written by a former servant of some well-known, or royal, subject.

video biography. Pictorial lives on cassette tapes, usually with a narrator who gives an account of the life accompanying the motion picture excerpts. Such lives are inevitably of outstanding persons whose lives have been photographed at various times on film. The Video Library of Biography, with narration by Mike Wallace, includes over twenty ninety-minute cassettes on subjects from Teddy Roosevelt and Gandhi to John Glenn and Grace Kelly.

vignette. In photography or portraiture a vignette is a picture showing only the head and upper part of the body, shading off gradually rather than having a definite border. In biography it has a meaning similar to that of **silhouette, sketch,** or **profile**—a brief portraiture presenting only outstanding features of the subject but suggesting the background into which they merge.

vituperative biography. Lives that reveal the hostility of biographer to subject; abusive lives. Although the large proportion of lives are sympathetically commemorative, there are occasionally antagonistic lives, sometimes notorious, written from a motivation for destruction of reputation, or perhaps merely out of a spirit of personal revenge; the oxymoron "vindictive hagiography" has been applied to this type. One of the most well-known and earliest vituperative biographies is Thomas More's *Richard III* (written about 1513; pub. 1557), which influenced the public conception of King Richard's character for centuries (largely through Shakespeare). Political lives (e.g., Robert Caro's *Mean Ascent: The Years of Lyndon Johnson,* 1990) as well as literary lives (e.g., Rufus Griswold on Poe) can be classed as vituperative.

voyages. Journey by sea or water, from one place to another, usually to some distant place or country; a course, or spell, of navigation or sailing; a cruise; in modern times, a flight through the air (or space); a balloon trip. Early accounts of travels often took the form of voyages, especially in the period of extensive explorations, the late sixteenth and the seventeenth centuries. The most famous and surely one of the most extensive such accounts is Richard Hakluyt, *Principall Navigations, Voiages, and Discoveries of the English Nation,* 1589, and, much enlarged, in three volumes, 1598–1600. See **autobiography, diary, tour, travels, Wanderjahr.**

W

Wanderjahr. (Ger., "travel year"). Autobiographical works that often contain, or are restricted to, youthful years of travel. Although the term originally applied to artisans or apprentices, who spent a year or more traveling before settling down in one place, the term has taken on a wider application, comparable in a way to *Bildungsroman* (novel of youth growing into maturity), referring to any life story that deals with a youthful period of travel and adventure (e.g., Richard Henry Dana, Jr., *Two Years Before the Mast,* 1840). See **tour, travels.**

"warts and all." Originally "wart and all," from Oliver Cromwell's directions to his portrait painter ("Paint me wart and all"); often used in reviews of noneulogistic biographies that leave out very little, usually used in a complimentary sense. See **hackiography.**

Wheel of Fortune. An image or figurative expression, an emblem of mutability or change, particularly popular in medieval literature; the "decline of princes," "the fall of great men." One of the best examples of this symbol used in a life story is George Cavendish's *The Life and Death of Cardinal Wolsey,* first printed in 1641, but long before that circulated in manuscript. See **fall.**

Who's Who. A modern biographical dictionary that concerns itself with eminent living persons; published at regular intervals, it gives brief biographical sketches of those who have been outstanding in their fields. *Who's Who* is a British publication, paralleled in the U.S.A. by *Who's Who in America;* supplemented in recent years by *Who Was Who,* which gives complete lives of those now deceased who were included in *Who's Who.* There are many biographical dictionaries patterned after these originals, covering prominent persons in more limited areas, such as professions, groups, or regional areas. See **biographical dictionary.**

widow biography. A biography written by a subject's widow; a pejorative term used by Harold Nicolson to reflect on the surviving family's desire to praise a famous man and to hide his faults. Edmund Gosse, in 1903, calls the widow as biographer "an instance of the survival of the unfittest in biographical literature." A remarkable example of the problem of the widow life-writer is that of Thomas Hardy, whose second wife and widow, Florence E. Hardy, was chosen by him to be the author of his official life, but he dictated and wrote most of the biography. See Michael Millgate's *Testamentary Acts* (1992) and *The Life and Work of Thomas Hardy,* by Thomas Hardy, edited by Michael Millgate (1985), which reveals the parts of that life of Hardy written by the widow.

wills. Legal statements made by persons indicating their wishes concerning disposal of property after death. Next to letters, diaries, and journals, wills may be the most significant documents available to the biographer. Not all subjects of biography leave a will, but the study of wills (see an entertaining account in *Wills: A Dead Giveaway,* 1974, by Millie Considine and Ruth Pool) indicates how frequently important aspects of character or significant factual material may be discovered in these personal documents (witness the name "Ellen Ternan" in Dickens' will). See **documentation, scholarly biography, testamentary acts.**

works. A person's writings or compositions as a whole; works of art, or literary or musical works. Biographies of literary men often stress their writings as well as the events in their lives; in the nineteenth century a title such as *Life and Works* is common; it may or may not mean a biography and an edition of the literary figure's writings or an anthology from the author's works; it may mean only a consideration of the works along with the facts of the life story. See **life.**

worthies. Distinguished or eminent persons; famous or renowned men and women; especially people of noble character, often individuals of courage or heroes of antiquity. In Britain the term is used more often and more seriously than in the U.S.A. One of the most famous collections of such lives is Thomas Fuller's *The Worthies of England* (1662). The Nine Worthies were nine famous ancient and medieval men of history and legend, sometimes called the Nine Nobles: three Jews (Joshua, David, Judas Maccabaeus), three Gentiles (Hector, Alexander, Julius Caesar), and three Christians (Arthur, Charlemagne, Godfrey of Bouillon). In modern times the word "worthies" may be used half-humorously or ironically. See **hero, multibiography.**

Books on Life-Writing

THE FOLLOWING LIST is made up of some of the works cited in the preceding definitions and of general books on biography and autobiography, especially from recent years. There were very few book-length studies on life-writing before the present century, and although many essays, particularly by Thomas Carlyle, were written on biography in the nineteenth century, eighteenth century essays by Samuel Johnson remain among the best comments on life-writing in any period. Some of the following books are collections of such essays. Since 1978 the periodical *Biography: An Interdisciplinary Quarterly* has carried in its Fall issue an annual bibliography of books and articles about life-writing.

Aaron, Daniel, ed. *Studies in Biography.* Harvard English Studies, No. 8. Cambridge: Harvard University Press, 1978.

a/b Auto/Biography Studies. Biannual journal published by the University of Kansas.

Addis, Patricia K. *Through a Woman's I: An Annotated Bibliography of American Women's Autobiographical Writings, 1946–1976.* Metuchen, NJ: Scarecrow, 1983.

Akeret, Robert U. *Photoanalysis: How to Interpret the Hidden Psychological Meaning of Personal and Public Photographs.* New York: Pocket Books, 1975.

Altick, Richard D. *Lives and Letters: A History of Literary Biography in England and America.* New York: Alfred A. Knopf, 1965.

Alvarez, A. *The Savage God: A Study of Suicide.* London: Weidenfeld and Nicolson, 1971.

Andrews, William L. *To Tell a Free Story: The First Century of Afro-American Autobiography, 1760–1865.* Urbana: University of Illinois Press, 1986.

Arksey, Laura, Nancy Pries, and Marcia Reed, comps. *American Diaries: An Annotated Bibliography of Published American Diaries.* Volume 1. *Diaries Written from 1492 to 1844.* Detroit: Gale, 1983.

Auto/Biography. Biannual Bulletin of the British Sociological Association Study Group on Auto/Biography.

Balch, Marston, ed. *Modern Short Biographies and Autobiographies.* New York: Harcourt Brace, 1935.

Bates, E. Stuart. *Inside Out: An Introduction to Autobiography.* New York: Sheridan House, 1937.

Bayliss, John F. *Black Slave Narratives.* New York: Macmillan, 1970.

Blasing, Mutlu Konuk. *The Art of Life: Studies in American Autobiographical Literature.* Austin: University of Texas Press, 1977.

Botkin, B. A., ed. *Lay My Burden Down: A Folk History of Slavery.* Athens: University of Georgia Press, 1989.

Bottrall, Margaret. *Every Man a Phoenix: Studies in Seventeenth Century Autobiography.* London: J. Murray, 1958.

Bowen, Catherine Drinker. *Biography: The Craft and the Calling.* Boston: Little, Brown, 1969.

Boyce, Benjamin. *The Theophrastan Character.* Cambridge: Harvard University Press, 1947.

Bradford, Gamaliel. *Biography and the Human Heart.* Boston: Houghton Mifflin, 1932.

Brady, John. *The Craft of Interviewing.* Cincinnati: Writer's Digest, 1976.

Braudy, Leo. *The Frenzy of Renown: Fame and Its History.* New York: Oxford University Press, 1986.

Brignano, Russell C. *Black America in Autobiography: An Annotated Bibliography of Autobiographies and Autobiographical Books Written Since the Civil War.* Durham: Duke University Press, 1974.

Brilliant, Richard. *Portraiture.* Cambridge: Harvard University Press, 1991.

Briscoe, Mary Louise, Barbara Tobias, and Lynn Z. Bloom, comps. *American Autobiography, 1945–1980: A Bibliography.* Madison: University of Wisconsin Press, 1982.

Britt, Albert. *The Great Biographers.* New York: McGraw-Hill, 1936.

Brown, William Burlie. *The People's Choice: The Presidential Image in the Campaign Biography.* Baton Rouge: Louisiana State University Press, 1960.

Brumble, H. David, III, comp. *An Annotated Bibliography of American Indian and Eskimo Autobiographies.* Lincoln: University of Nebraska Press, 1981.

Bruss, Elizabeth W. *Autobiographical Acts: The Changing Situation of a Literary Genre.* Baltimore: Johns Hopkins University Press, 1976.

Buckley, Jerome H., ed. *The Turning Key: Autobiography and the Subjective Impulse Since 1800.* Cambridge: Harvard University Press, 1984.

—————. *Nineteenth-Century Lives.* Cambridge: Cambridge University Press, 1989.

Burr, Anna Robeson. *The Autobiography: A Critical and Comparative Study.* Boston: Houghton Mifflin, 1909.

Butterfield, Stephen. *Black Autobiography in America.* Amherst: University of Massachusetts Press, 1974.

Carver, George. *Alms For Oblivion: Books, Men and Biography.* Milwaukee: Bruce, 1946.

Clark, Arthur M. *Autobiography: Its Genesis and Phases.* Edinburgh: Oliver and Boyd, 1935.

Clifford, James L., ed. *Biography As an Art: Selected Criticism 1560–1960.* New York: Oxford University Press, 1962.

—————. *From Puzzles to Portraits: Problems of a Literary Biographer.* Chapel Hill: University of North Carolina Press, 1970.

Cockshut, A. O. J. *Truth to Life: The Art of Biography in the Nineteenth Century.* London: Collins, 1974.

—————. *The Art of Autobiography in Nineteenth- and Twentieth-Century England.* New Haven: Yale University Press, 1984.

Collins, Joseph. *The Doctor Looks at Biography.* New York: Doran, 1925.

Connely, Willard. *Adventures in Biography.* London: Laurie, 1956.

Cooley, Thomas. *Educated Lives: The Rise of Modern Autobiography in America.* Columbus: Ohio State University Press, 1976.

Couser, G. Thomas. *American Autobiography: The Prophetic Mode.* Amherst: University of Massachusetts Press, 1979.

Cox, James M. *Recovering Literature's Lost Ground: Essays in American Autobiography.* Baton Rouge: Louisiana State University Press, 1989.

Cross, Wilbur L. *An Outline of Biography: From Plutarch to Strachey.* New York: Holt, 1924.

Culley, Margo, ed. *A Day at a Time: The Diary Literature of American Women: From 1764 to the Present.* New York: Feminist Press, 1986.

Daghlian, Philip B., ed. *Essays in Eighteenth-Century Biography.* Bloomington: Indiana University Press, 1968.

Dargan, Marion. *A Guide to American Biography.* Albuquerque: University of New Mexico, 1949.

Davis, Charles T. and Henry L. Gates, Jr., eds. *The Slave's Narrative.* New York: Oxford University Press, 1985.

Davis, Cullom, Kathryn Back, and Kay MacLean. *Oral History: From Tape to Type.* Chicago: American Library Association, 1977.

Delany, Paul. *British Autobiography in the Seventeenth Century.* London: Routledge and Kegan Paul, 1969.

D'Emilio, John. *Making Trouble: Essays on Gay History, Politics, and the University.* New York: Routledge, 1992.

Dixon, Janice T. and Dora D. Flack. *Preserving Your Past: A Painless Guide to Writing Your Autobiography and Family History.* New York: Doubleday, 1977.

Dorey, T. A., ed. *Latin Biography.* London: Routledge and Kegan Paul, 1967.

Drew, Elizabeth. *The Literature of Gossip: Nine English Letter Writers.* New York: W. W. Norton, 1964.

Dudley, David L. *My Father's Shadow: Intergenerational Conflict in African American Men's Autobiography.* Philadelphia: University of Pennsylvania Press, 1991.

Dunn, Waldo H. *English Biography.* London: Dent; New York: Dutton, 1916.

Eakin, Paul J. *Fictions in Autobiography: Studies in the Art of Self-Invention.* Princeton: Princeton University Press, 1985.

—————. *Touching the World: Reference in Autobiography.* Princeton: Princeton University Press, 1992.

Earle, William. *The Autobiographical Consciousness: A Philosophical Inquiry into Existence.* Chicago: Quadrangle, 1972.

Ebner, Dean. *Autobiography in Seventeenth-Century England: Theology and the Self.* The Hague: Mouton, 1971.

Edel, Leon. *Literary Biography.* Toronto: University of Toronto Press, 1957.

—————. *Writing Lives: Principia Biographica.* New York: W. W. Norton, 1984.

Egan, Susannah. *Patterns of Experience in Autobiography.* Chapel Hill: University of North Carolina Press, 1984.

Ellmann, Richard. *Eminent Domain: Yeats Among Wilde, Joyce, Pound, Eliot and Auden.* New York: Oxford University Press, 1967.
————. *Literary Biography.* London: Oxford University Press, 1971.
————. *Golden Codgers: Biographical Speculations.* New York: Oxford University Press, 1973.
Epstein, William H., ed. *Recognizing Biography.* Philadelphia: University of Pennsylvania Press, 1987.
————. *Contesting the Subject: Essays in the Postmodern Theory and Practice of Biography and Biographical Criticism.* West Lafayette: Purdue University Press, 1991.
Fleishman, Avrom. *Figures of Autobiography: The Language of Self-Writing in Victorian and Modern England.* Berkeley and Los Angeles: University of California Press, 1983.
Forbes, Harriette M. *New England Diaries: 1602–1800: A Descriptive Catalogue of Diaries, Orderly Books, and Sea Journals.* New York: Russell and Russell, 1967.
Foster, Frances S. *Witnessing Slavery: The Development of Ante-Bellum Slave Narratives.* Westport, CT: Greenwood, 1979.
————. *Written by Herself, Literary Production by African American Women, 1746–1892.* Bloomington: Indiana University Press, 1993.
Fothergill, Robert A. *Private Chronicles: A Study of English Diaries.* London: Oxford University Press, 1974.
Friedson, Anthony M., ed. *New Directions in Biography.* A Biography Monograph. Honolulu: University of Hawai'i Press, 1981.
Garraty, John A. *The Nature of Biography.* New York: Alfred A. Knopf, 1970.
Gittelson, Celia. *Biography.* New York: Alfred A. Knopf, 1991.
Gittings, Robert. *The Nature of Biography.* Seattle: University of Washington Press, 1978.
Golden, Morris. *The Self Observed: Swift, Johnson, Wordsworth.* Baltimore: Johns Hopkins University Press, 1972.
Gosse, Edmund. *Tallemant des Réaux or the Art of Miniature in Biography.* Oxford: Clarendon, 1925.
Gunn, Janet V. *Autobiography: Toward a Poetics of Experience.* Philadelphia, University of Pennsylvania Press, 1982.
Heilbrun, Carolyn G. *Writing a Woman's Life.* New York: W. W. Norton, 1988.
Hoberman, Ruth. *Modernizing Lives: Experiments in English Biography, 1918–1939.* Carbondale: Southern Illinois University Press, 1987.
Hoffman, Leonore and Margo Culley, eds. *Women's Personal Narratives: Essays in Criticism and Pedagogy.* New York: Modern Language Association, 1985.
Honan, Park. *Authors' Lives: On Literary Biography and the Arts of Language.* New York: St. Martin's, 1990.
Hood, Edwin Paxton. *The Uses of Biography: Romantic, Philosophic, Didactic.* London: Partridge and Oakey, 1852.
Houser, G. Thomas. *American Autobiography: The Prophetic Mode.* Amherst: University of Massachusetts Press, 1979.
Huff, Cynthia. *British Women's Diaries: A Descriptive Bibliography of Selected Nineteenth-Century Women's Manuscript Diaries.* New York: AMS, 1985.

Irwin, Theodore. *How Weather and Climate Affect You.* Public Affairs Pamphlet No. 533. New York: Public Affairs Committee, 1976.

James, Edward T., Janet W. James, and Paul S. Boyer, eds. *Notable American Women, 1607–1950: A Biographical Dictionary.* 3 volumes. Cambridge: Harvard University Press, 1971.

Jelinek, Estelle C. *The Tradition of Women's Autobiography: From Antiquity to the Present.* Boston: Twayne, 1986.

Johnson, Edgar. *One Mighty Torrent: The Drama of Biography.* New York: Macmillan, 1937, 1955.

—————. *A Treasury of Biography.* New York: Howell, Soskin, 1941.

Johnston, James C. *Biography: The Literature of Personality.* New York: Century, 1927.

Jones, A. H. M., J. R. Martindale, and J. Morris. *The Prosopography of the Later Roman Empire.* Volume 1. *260–395.* Cambridge: Cambridge University Press, 1971.

Jones, Charles W. *Saints' Lives and Chronicles in Early England.* Ithaca: Cornell University Press, 1947.

Jones, George J. and E. F. Sleman. *History in Biography.* Boston: Heath, 1939.

Kagle, Steven E. *American Diary Literature, 1620–1799.* Boston: Twayne, 1979.

Kaplan, Louis. *A Bibliography of American Autobiographies.* Madison: University of Wisconsin Press, 1962.

Kendall, Paul M. *The Art of Biography.* New York: W. W. Norton, 1965.

Landow, George P., ed. *Approaches to Victorian Autobiography.* Athens: Ohio University Press, 1979.

Lee, Sidney. *Principles of Biography.* New York: Macmillan, 1911.

Lewis, C. S. and E. M. W. Tillyard. *The Personal Heresy: A Controversy.* London: Oxford University Press, 1939.

Lillard, Richard G. *American Life in Autobiography: A Descriptive Guide.* Stanford: Stanford University Press, 1956.

Longaker, Mark. *English Biography in the Eighteenth Century.* Philadelphia: University of Pennsylvania Press, 1931.

—————. *Contemporary Biography.* Philadelphia: University of Pennsylvania Press, 1934.

Major, John C. *The Role of Personal Memoirs in English Biography and Novel.* Philadelphia: University of Pennsylvania Press, 1935.

Mandell, Gail Porter. *Life into Art: Conversations with Seven Contemporary Biographers.* Fayetteville: University of Arkansas Press, 1991.

Matthews, William, comp. *American Diaries: An Annotated Bibliography of American Diaries Written Prior to the Year 1861.* Berkeley and Los Angeles: University of California Press, 1945.

—————. *British Autobiographies: An Annotated Bibliography of British Autobiographies Published or Written Before 1951.* Berkeley and Los Angeles: University of California Press, 1955.

—————. *British Diaries: An Annotated Bibliography of British Diaries Written Between 1442 and 1942.* Berkeley and Los Angeles: University of California Press, 1950.

Marwick, Arthur. *The Nature of History.* New York: Alfred A. Knopf, 1970.

Maurois, André. *Aspects of Biography.* New York: Appleton, 1929.

Mehlman, Jeffrey. *A Structural Study of Autobiography: Proust, Leiris, Sartre, Lévi-Strauss.* Ithaca: Cornell University Press, 1974.

Merrill, Dana K. *American Biography: Its Theory and Practice.* Portland, ME: Southworth, 1932.

Mersand, Joseph. *A Decade of Biographical Plays, 1928–38.* New York: Modern Chap Books, 1939.

Meyers, Jeffrey, ed. *The Craft of Literary Biography.* New York: Schocken, 1985.

————. *Biographers's Art.* New York: New Amsterdam, 1989.

————. *The Spirit of Biography.* Ann Arbor: University of Michigan Press, 1989.

Millgate, Michael. *Testamentary Acts.* Oxford: Clarendon, 1992.

Misch, Georg. *A History of Autobiography in Antiquity.* Tr. E. W. Dickes (first published in German, 1907). 2 volumes. Cambridge: Harvard University Press, 1949, 1950.

Momigliano, Arnaldo. *The Development of Greek Biography.* Cambridge: Harvard University Press, 1971.

Moraitis, George and George H. Pollock, eds. *Psychoanalytic Studies of Biography.* Madison, CT: International Universities Press, 1987.

Morris, John N. *Versions of the Self: Studies in English Autobiography from John Bunyan to John Stuart Mill.* New York: Basic Books, 1966.

Nadel, Ira Bruce. *Biography: Fiction, Fact and Form.* New York: St. Martin's, 1984.

Nicolson, Harold. *The Development of English Biography.* London: Hogarth, 1927.

Novarr, David. *The Making of Walton's Lives.* Ithaca: Cornell University Press, 1958.

————. *The Lines of Life: Theories of Biography, 1880–1970.* West Lafayette: Purdue University Press, 1986.

Oates, Stephen B., ed. *Biography as High Adventure: Life-Writers Speak on Their Art.* Amherst: University of Massachusetts Press, 1986.

Ober, William B. *Boswell's Clap and Other Essays: Medical Analyses of Literary Men's Afflictions.* Carbondale: Southern Illinois University Press, 1979.

————. *Bottoms Up! A Pathologist's Essays on Medicine and the Humanities.* Carbondale: Southern Illinois University Press, 1987.

O'Brien, Kate. *English Diaries and Journals.* London: Collins, 1943.

Olney, James, ed. *Metaphors of Self: The Meaning of Autobiography.* Princeton: Princeton University Press, 1972.

————. *Autobiography: Essays Theoretical and Critical.* Princeton: Princeton University Press, 1980.

————. *Studies in Autobiography.* New York: Oxford University Press, 1988.

O'Neill, Edward H. *A History of American Biography 1800–1935.* Philadelphia: University of Pennsylvania Press, 1935; New York: A. S. Barnes, 1961.

Osborn, James. *The Beginnings of Autobiography in England.* Los Angeles: William Andrews Clark Memorial Library, University of California at Los Angeles, 1959.

Pachter, Marc, ed. *Telling Lives: The Biographer's Art.* Washington, D.C.: New Republic, 1979.

Pascal, Roy. *Design and Truth in Autobiography.* Cambridge: Harvard University Press, 1960.

Pearson, Hesketh. *Ventilations, Being Biographical Asides.* Philadelphia: Lippincott, 1930.

Peterson, Linda H. *Victorian Autobiography: The Tradition of Self-Interpretation.* New Haven: Yale University Press, 1986.

Petrie, Dennis W. *Ultimately Fiction: Design in Modern American Literary Biography.* West Lafayette: Purdue University Press. 1981.

Pickering, George. *Creative Malady: Illness in the Lives and Minds of Charles Darwin, Florence Nightingale, Mary Baker Eddy, Sigmund Freud, Marcel Proust, Elizabeth Barrett Browning.* New York: Oxford University Press, 1974.

Pilling, John. *Autobiography and Imagination: Studies in Self-Scrutiny.* London: Routledge and Kegan Paul, 1981.

Piper, David. *The English Face.* London: National Portrait Gallery, 1978.

Ponsonby, Arthur. *English Diaries.* London: Methuen, 1923.

—————. *More English Diaries.* London: Methuen, 1927.

—————. *Scottish and Irish Diaries.* London: Methuen, 1927.

Pottle, Frederick A. *The Literary Career of James Boswell Esq.* Oxford: Clarendon, 1929, 1965.

—————. *Pride and Negligence: The History of the Boswell Papers.* New York: McGraw-Hill, 1982.

Reed, Joseph W. Jr. *English Biography in the Early Nineteenth Century, 1801–1838.* New Haven: Yale University Press, 1966.

Rees, Nigel. *Epitaphs: A Dictionary of Grave Epigrams and Memorial Eloquence.* London: Bloomsbury, 1993.

Reid, B. L. *Necessary Lives: Biographical Reflections.* Columbia: University of Missouri Press, 1990.

Rewa, Michael P. *Reborn as Meaning: Panegyrical Biography from Isocrates to Walton.* Washington, D.C.: University Press of America, 1983.

Rhodes, Carolyn H. *First Person Female American: A Selected and Annotated Bibliography of the Autobiographies of American Women Living After 1950.* Troy, NY: Whitston, 1980.

Riches, Phyllis. *An Analytical Bibliography of Universal Collected Biographies.* London: Library Association, 1934.

Rosen, Stephen. *Weathering: How Our Atmosphere Conditions Your Body, Your Mind, Your Moods—and Your Health.* New York: M. Evans, 1979.

Sayre, Robert F. *The Examined Self: Benjamin Franklin, Henry Adams, Henry James.* Princeton: Princeton University Press, 1964.

Schellinger, Paul E., ed. *St. James Guide to Biography.* Chicago: St. James, 1991.

Schlissel, Lillian. *Women's Diaries of the Westward Journey.* New York: Schocken, 1982.

Schwartz, Richard B. *Boswell's Johnson: A Preface to the "Life."* Madison: University of Wisconsin Press, 1978.

Shea, Daniel B. Jr. *Spiritual Autobiography in Early America.* Princeton: Princeton University Press, 1968.

Shelston, Alan. *Biography.* No. 34 in the Critical Idiom series. London: Methuen, 1977.

Shumaker, Wayne. *English Autobiography: Its Emergence, Materials, and Form.* Berkeley and Los Angeles: University of California Press, 1954.

Slocum, Robert B, ed. *Biographical Dictionaries and Related Works.* Detroit: Gale, 1978.

Smith, Sidonie. *Where I'm Bound: Patterns of Slavery and Freedom in Black American Autobiography.* Westport, CT: Greenwood, 1974.

Spacks, Patricia M. *Imagining a Self: Autobiography and Novel in Eighteenth-Century England.* Cambridge: Harvard University Press, 1976.

—————. *Gossip.* New York: Alfred A. Knopf, 1985.

Spalding, P. A. *Self Harvest: A Study of Diaries and the Diarist.* London: Independent, 1949.

Spengemann, William C. *The Forms of Autobiography: Episodes in the History of a Literary Genre.* New Haven: Yale University Press, 1980.

Stanton, Donna C. *The Female Autograph.* New York: New York Literary Forum, 1984.

Stauffer, Donald A. *English Biography Before 1700.* Cambridge: Harvard University Press, 1930.

—————. *The Art of Biography in Eighteenth-Century England* (with a separate volume *Bibliographical Supplement*). Princeton: Princeton University Press, 1941.

Stephen, Leslie. *Studies of a Biographer.* 4 volumes. London: Duckworth, 1898, 1902, 1907.

Stone, Albert E. *Autobiographical Occasions and Original Acts: Versions of American Identity from Henry Adams to Nate Shaw.* Philadelphia: University of Pennsylvania Press, 1982.

Strachey, G. Lytton. *Biographical Essays.* New York: Harcourt, Brace and World, 1969.

Stuart, Duane R. *Epochs of Greek and Roman Biography.* Berkeley and Los Angeles: University of California Press, 1928.

Sturrock, John. *The Language of Autobiography.* Cambridge: University of Cambridge Press, 1993.

Thayer, William Roscoe. *The Art of Biography.* New York: Scribners, 1920.

Thompson, Paul. *The Voice of the Past: Oral History.* Oxford: Oxford University Press, 1978.

Trevelyan, G. M. *Biography: A Reader's Guide.* London: National Book League, 1947.

Valentine, Alan C. *Biography.* Oxford Reading Courses. New York: Oxford University Press, 1927.

Weintraub, Karl J. *The Value of the Individual: Self and Circumstance in Autobiography.* Chicago: University of Chicago Press, 1978.

Wendorf, Richard. *The Elements of Life: Biography and Portrait-Painting in Stuart and Georgian England.* Oxford: Clarendon, 1990.

West, Andrew F. *Roman Autobiography.* New York: De Vinne, 1901.

Wethered, H. N. *The Curious Art of Autobiography from Benvenuto Cellini to Rudyard Kipling.* New York: Philosophical Library, 1956.

Whittemore, Reed. *Whole Lives: Shapers of Modern Biography.* Baltimore: Johns Hopkins University Press, 1989.

Woolf, Virginia. *Granite and Rainbow.* Part II: *The Art of Biography.* New York: Harcourt Brace, 1958.